The Seven Mountain Mantle takes its place as a core textbook for those of us who are focused on reforming our society. Johnny Enlow refuses to be bound by tired, old-wineskin stereotypes embedded in each mountain. Instead he projects fresh, new, creative approaches for immediate kingdom action. Please do not miss this dynamic new book! You'll regret it if you do!

—C. Peter Wagner
Chancellor, Wagner Leadership Institute

I love Johnny Enlow and his deep search for the deeper waters of the knowledge of God...*The Seven Mountain Mantle* is a powerful call straight from the heart of God to all Josephs in the marketplace and the body of Christ concerning the hopeful times and seasons we are in.

This book is one of the key doors to help take us from the room of despair to God's strategy room, which is filled with hope. There we gain a kingdom perspective that will help us see societies and nations that will love God well.

Johnny takes us on a journey of hoping in God as true Josephs in this prophetic hour. He opens up the knowledge of who God desires to be in and through us in this unique time...

I highly recommend Johnny and this book as a source that leads us into the purposes of God's heart for the body of Christ.

—Bob Hartley
President and CEO, Hartley Institute/Deeper Waters

Pastor Johnny Enlow's latest book, *The Seven Mountain Mantle*, is a sneak preview of how the reformation of nations could unfold if all across the globe the Lord's Josephs would arise, accept the call on their lives, and invade the mountains that influence culture. This book is packed with revelation that will inspire you as you identify your mountain. May the battle cry "Lord, give me my mountain" arise within you as you catch a glimpse of God's heart for our generation.

—Pastor Lisette Malmberg
Senior Pastor, New Life Tabernacle
President and Founder, The Kingdom Leadership Institute in Aruba

This new book of Johnny Enlow's, *The Seven Mountain Mantle*...is a kingdom book that will begin to shift the body of Christ into the seven mountain prophecy. God will not show us mountains without the strategy to take them. What you will read in this book will move us from the knowing to the taking. All I can say is it's time.

—Cal Pierce
International Director, Healing Rooms Ministries
Serve the City Foundation

It is one thing to know the importance of influencing society on every level and another to know how to do it God's way. Johnny Enlow once again shares insight we all need.

—Che Ahn
Senior Pastor, Harvest Rock Church
President, Harvest International Ministry

In ⟨barcode⟩ e heavenly Father's passion and divine wisdom
for ⟨barcode⟩ sectors of the society and ignites modern-day
Jos ⟨barcode⟩ minating!

—Dr. Shaun Wang
shed Professor of Actuarial Science
Chairman of Risk Lighthouse LLC

GW00492837

Johnny Enlow's *The Seven Mountain Mantle* is a riveting and worthy sequel to his first, ground-breaking book on this topic and provides a searing indictment of contemporary Christian culture in the West, marked by its foci on the gospel of salvation, escapist theology, and religion, and its limited impact and influence on societal culture. Far from being an intellectual critic who is emotionally detached from what he writes about, Enlow, as a devoted practitioner, disciple, and champion of the church, provides a cogent, compelling case for the church to change direction...and begin implementing, embracing, advocating, and modeling a kingdom culture marked by the gospel of the kingdom...

—DR. BRUCE COOK
PRESIDENT, KINGDOM HOUSE PUBLISHING

Johnny gives a powerful picture of believers whom God is raising up to bring change in the Earth. This prophetic message is vital for being equipped to participate in God's dream for the Earth. I highly recommend this very timely book.

—BARBARA WENTROBLE
PRESIDENT, INTERNATIONAL BREAKTHROUGH MINISTRIES

A masterful job of telling the age-old story of Joseph with relevance for the days we live in. Johnny has given us a prophetic, strategic insight and plan for the role of the church for this hour to reshape culture.

—OS HILLMAN
PRESIDENT, MARKETPLACE LEADERS

If your vision for the End Times consists of a small group of persecuted believers hiding out in caves, eating canned vegetables, and praying that the Antichrist won't nab them, this book is definitely not for you. In fact, reading it may even confuse you. You are holding an instruction manual for people who want to reform the system, not run away from it. If, however, your vision consists of infiltrating the world system and subjecting kingdoms of darkness to the righteousness, peace, and joy of a heavenly kingdom, I believe that you will find this book helpful. Read on and enjoy.

—CALEV MYERS
FOUNDER AND CHIEF COUNSEL OF THE JERUSALEM INSTITUTE OF JUSTICE

Johnny Enlow is one of the foremost prophets of our day. While most prophetic people in these troubled times think it's their responsibility to give an accurate commentary on the valley of dry bones, Johnny looks at the bones and calls forth a mighty army.

This book is filled with hope, inspires wisdom, and gives us answers for our time. The author digs deep into the lives of biblical characters like Joseph, Leah, and Rachel and unearths the lost treasure chest filled with stunning insights for the restoration of our broken cities. This book is a must read for all those who are tired of powerless Christianity and are ready to be a catalyst to cultural revolution.

—KRIS VALLOTTON
COFOUNDER, BETHEL SCHOOL OF SUPERNATURAL MINISTRY
SENIOR ASSOCIATE LEADER, BETHEL CHURCH, REDDING, CALIFORNIA

Information is nothing without strategy. God has commissioned us to transform the world. Johnny Enlow has laid out what is on God's heart and how we can do it His way. Powerful insight!

—LOU ENGLE
PRESIDENT OF THE CALL

The Seven Mountain Mantle

Johnny Enlow

CREATION
HOUSE
A STRANG COMPANY

THE SEVEN MOUNTAIN MANTLE by Johnny Enlow
Published by Creation House
A Strang Company
600 Rinehart Road
Lake Mary, Florida 32746
www.strangbookgroup.com

Unless otherwise noted, all Scripture quotations are from the New King James Version of the Bible. Copyright © 1979, 1980, 1982 by Thomas Nelson, Inc., publishers. Used by permission.

Scripture quotations marked NAS are from the New American Standard Bible. Copyright © 1960, 1962, 1963, 1968, 1971, 1972, 1973, 1975, 1977 by the Lockman Foundation. Used by permission. (www.Lockman.org)

Scripture quotations marked KJV are from the King James Version of the Bible.

Design Director: Bill Johnson
Cover design by Bill Johnson

Library of Congress Control Number: 2009937868
International Standard Book Number: 978-1-59979-963-6

10 11 12 13 — 9 8 7 6 5 4 3 2
Printed in the United States of America

This book is dedicated to the memory of my brother-in-law, Martin Crosson, who shared my passion for getting this message out to the nations.

Acknowledgments

I WOULD LIKE TO thank some very key people who have helped with this significant task of publishing a book. First of all I must acknowledge the invaluable assistance of my wife, Elizabeth, who provided tremendous input at every stage of this project. She is the most responsible for helping me make the time to write this book, and at every stage her ideas and advice have been noteworthy. She is my greatest cheerleader and best friend. This book comes out of the sum of who we are as a couple.

Next I would like to acknowledge the prayer and ongoing encouragement from the Daystar Church staff and members—particularly Chris Tiegreen for his editing expertise and wise counsel throughout the editing process and Amanda Ginn for her assistance and attention to details and deadlines. She has been greatly responsible for the practical efforts surrounding getting this revelation out to the nations. Elizabeth and I have appreciated the ways our associate pastors, Kevin and Rachel Dyck, have stepped into greater responsibilities so that we could be better stewards of this message. The Daystar members who serve the Father with us have been such a constant encouragement as I have learned to communicate the fresh things of the Spirit.

I am also grateful to my prayer warrior mother, Gladys Enlow, and Karen Ruff, chief intercessor at Daystar, and her faithful team, for the authority they pray with because of the humility they walk in. Lastly I would like to honor my daughters, family, and in-laws for celebrating with me all that God is doing on this adventure!

Contents

Foreword

THOUGH I FIRST recognized my need for a Savior more than thirty-five years ago, it wasn't until just a few months ago that I addressed what I had learned to ignore so well—what I now refer to as "the pink elephant in the room" of my soul. I had finally realized that I didn't trust God and in fact hated Him! It was the middle of the night, and my forever-patient and compassionate husband held me as I let God know how much I hated Him, how evil He was, and that He should definitely not be trusted.

This is a very inconvenient truth to realize, especially when you're a pastor! Not sure if Johnny would quickly relieve me of all pastoral responsibilities at Daystar, the words he spoke to me through my intense sobs of pain and anger profoundly ministered to me. Although I could share with you the circumstances that surfaced around my trust issues with God, the details aren't necessary—we all have gone or will go through a detailed, tailor-made process designed to push every control button we may have if we have ever expressed any desire to God to grow spiritually. I'll just put it this way: I was put in a position in which I needed to trust God in a new way, and that sent shock waves through me all the way back to a time of such deep pain and disappointment that I finally had to be honest with Him.

If you have never gone to that dreaded place yourself, I can tell you that it's actually better than you can imagine—such freedom and new intimacy with God. I have found that He can take it and that I'm not too complicated for Him. The words my husband shared with me helped me feel a closeness to Jesus like never before. He reminded me that as He was dying on the cross, Jesus—fully God, yet limited to the same flesh as we are—also doubted the goodness of our Father. He quoted Psalm 22:1: "My God, My God, why have You forsaken Me?" Even Jesus, who was so close to God, wrongly perceived God in that moment of testing.

David, who originally expressed the feeling of that psalm, showed a pattern of honesty with God throughout his life about what he really felt, something I think most believers in our generation still need to learn. God already knows what we are struggling with, of course, but for our own sake we must determine to tear down everything that hinders love. For those who find the grace to embrace the path that all Josephs must walk, you will be amazed at how intricately your personal place of trust in God is related to the biggest picture of all—the kingdom of God established on Earth.

I've always thought that I would just leave the End Times to those who have time to study all those charts. All I cared about was doing what I'm supposed to do until I die or until Christ returns; explanations about the End Times seemed so confusing, anyway. But I have to admit that after hearing Johnny preach more times than I can recall on how Christians are called to bring the solutions of heaven to the problems in our nations through all seven areas of culture, I began to wonder how this is all going to play out. What will the end result be? What exactly are we working toward here? What is this war actually over, and how will we know when it's been won? When I was finally able to get honest with God and allow Him to talk to me about my pain and disappointments, I understood our role as a generation in the End Times more than I thought possible. I've discovered that the seven mountain revelation is more relevant to us than nearly anything else I've ever heard preached. Through my personal breakthrough with the Lord, He began to unfold to me some truths that I think will help you more fully digest and apply what you will learn in these pages.

We've all heard the story of the fateful day when Adam and Eve ate of the one tree that God told them not to eat from, the tree of the knowledge of good and evil. In that moment in time, the ones who had walked so intimately with God and knew Him face to face with no guilt, shame, or fear were suddenly no better off than all of the rest of us trying to figure out how to relate to our God. They knew *how* to be intimate with Him, yet still they *felt* distant from Him—distant enough to hide and look for a way to cover themselves. The fruit of that tree was obviously supernatural, and when eaten, it supernaturally changed their DNA and that of all humans after them. That change gave them and us the ability to question if something or someone is good or evil, and more specifically to question if *God* is good or evil.

I know it was sin that separated Adam and Eve from God, but I think there's more to what happened in the Garden of Eden. My theory is that most humans believe in their core that God *exists*, but we aren't so sure that He is *good*. We doubt His goodness and how much He really cares about us. We wonder if He cares about the things we care about. Johnny says it this way: "On the day they ate of that tree, they began to judge God." So my question to God was, "Why did You give them access to the tree if the results would be so horrific? Why allow us to get into a position of such doubt that we would undermine our ability to trust You and therefore lose our intimacy with You?" God began to speak to me about relationships and how, in order for true intimacy to happen, there must be a mutual, voluntary loss of control. What I mean by "loss of control" is the reality we experience when circumstances remind us that we ultimately can't control things. We forget that God has also voluntarily limited Himself to that same reality as it relates to us. In order for true intimacy to exist, both people must choose to give the other the option to disappoint them. Incredible risk brings the potential for incredible trust, which then produces the possibility for real intimacy. You can't have intimacy without trust, and you can't have trust without both people experiencing loss of control. In order to ultimately have the intimacy He desired to have with His sons and daughters, God had to give up some significant control by giving us the option to sin—eating of the tree of the knowledge of good and evil, achieving the ability to question His true nature or goodness.

So all this fuss is over God's desire to be close to His creation in a way we will probably only really understand when we see Him face to face. As we live this life, it becomes necessary to resolve this inner doubt over the goodness of God, and that can only happen as we realize this: because of that little "DNA glitch" that happened in the garden, these brains are wired to think that we can correctly perceive whether God is good or not based on the *circumstances we go through.* But the goodness of the Lord can only be tasted of and seen by intimacy through the spiritual realm, because He is spirit. Like Jesus' limitation—perceiving His Father's distance, when in reality God couldn't have been more proud of His only perfect Son—we too cannot correctly perceive God's heart toward us from this earthly vessel's fallen way of perceiving. We can be honest about the feelings of doubt, but as Jesus expressed in His final words on Earth, we must resolve to trust and say like Him, "Into Your hands I commit My spirit." In other words, "I *will* trust you!"

So what does our personal intimacy with God have to do with Joseph? What does Joseph have to do with us, other than some obvious lessons we can learn from his life? As you navigate through new prophetic insights God has given Johnny specifically for our generation, you will realize how specifically Joseph's heart of trust toward God tied into his eventual task of saving the world as he knew it. As He did with Joseph, God wants to use your intimacy with Him, your personal conviction that His true character is good, to save our world!

Remember in Matthew 25 when Jesus describes how one day all the nations will be gathered before Him and He will separate them like sheep from goats? He goes on to tell how the righteous sheep nations will be delineated from the goat nations based on whether they gave Him food and drink when He was hungry and thirsty, took Him in when He was a stranger, clothed Him when He was naked, visited Him when He was sick, and came to see Him in prison. They then ask, "When were you hungry or thirsty? When were you a stranger or naked?" Jesus says that He will then answer, "Inasmuch as you did it to one of the least of these My brethren, you did it to Me" (Matt. 25:40). Basically Jesus is equating Himself with "the least of these."

There is much more to this passage, but the main point I want to help you see in a new light is this: more than God is giving us a to-do list for the End Times, He is giving us a big hint that He is good. His heart is so on our side that He identifies Himself with the most needy among us. He also gives us a clue about what the war is really about. The war is not about who can perform good deeds the best; too many other scriptures clarify that salvation is not from works. The war is not about God needing to defeat Satan, because that already happened. It is not even over how many souls will be saved. I believe the war is over the truth of who God *really* is. His true nature will be displayed through the righteous, compassionate acts of Josephs who, because they trust their God, endure the journey from dreams of destiny, through seasons of what seem like demotions and unfair "prison sentences," to the reality of God supernaturally placing them into positions of influence and service in order to save our world and receive His kingdom!

In this End Time description of how we will be judged that Jesus gives us in Matthew, He reveals that God cares way more than we think He does. This is so important to get because we have an innate tendency in us to think, at least subconsciously, "Why care more than God does?" The problem is that we misjudge how much He cares and what He cares about. He says it so plainly there. He cares about even the least among us. That's how good and righteous He really is, and if we don't know that about Him, how will we ever correctly portray that to the world? Our life circumstances and our interpretation of them have misled all of us into wrong beliefs about God's true heart, so the ultimate expression of His people must be to restore back to the nations the reality of His goodness.

But there's more. This God who desires unhindered communion with us has an enemy. And that enemy is so pitiful that there's no match between him and God. So what does an enemy do to Someone he loathes so deeply but cannot touch? He goes after the object of God's affection—you and me. And how do you bring pain to a father's heart? Make his children believe his heart toward them is evil rather than good; make them believe lies about his true nature or character and convince them he can't be trusted; make them believe it on an individual level to such a degree that it plays out in the very culture of their nations. Because we don't know the *real* God, it shows in the foundations of our economy, education, families, religion, arts and entertainment, government, and media. Every area of our culture seems to send a message that undermines God's true nature, exalting our ways as better than His.

So not only did Satan tempt Adam and Eve into a choice that caused us to forever doubt God's goodness, thus undermining trust and intimacy with Him, but he also continues the war by using the very cultures of the world to defame God's true character. He attacks individually and on a global level. Therefore, we must be convinced that this war over the true identity of a God who is good must be waged on an individual level as well as on a worldwide level. This is our quest—to be personally convinced of God's goodness to such a degree that we display it in the nations through every place of cultural influence.

This task is too great for us, of course. But God, like any good Father, gave us more "stake in the game" than we really should have so that when the victory is fully seen, we will rejoice *with* Him as much as we rejoice *for*

Him! As much as your kids love you, they are never as excited for you as when they have participated with you in a victory. God doesn't just want a happy ending, He wants a celebration!

When I first read this manuscript, I wasn't prepared for the amount of hope that came rushing into my spiritual lungs. It was like I had gotten used to living on polluted air for so long that I had forgotten how vital hope is to us as believers. I'm convinced that in reading *The Seven Mountain Mantle: Receiving the Joseph Anointing to Reform Nations*, you too will drink deeply of a hope that is critical for those who intend not just to survive but to thrive in the days to come. I pray that as you move forward in reading and applying this prophetic message, you will dare to believe that you are a part of a generation of Josephs destined by God to access the solutions of heaven for whatever problems He gives you favor to solve. Dare to believe that He really does care!

May you be infused with such hope and faith that you are consumed with new focus and zeal to show forth the true identity of our God.

—ELIZABETH ENLOW

Introduction

Years ago, Loren Cunningham of Youth With a Mission and Bill Bright of Campus Crusade for Christ were on the way to meet each other when God gave each of them a revelation—a "seven mountain strategy" for shaping a nation. The Lord told them that there were seven "mountains" or mind-molders of society: media, education, government, economy/business, celebration of arts, religion, and family. He promised them that if God's people could capture these mountains, they could capture a nation.

A few years ago, God began giving me further revelations and insights on these mountains—the demonic spirits that hold them captive, the strategies for how God wants His people to ascend these mountains, and the favor He is going to give them for doing so. I saw in my spirit a revolution, "Elijahs" who would invade these sectors of society, not to control them by force but to displace the ruling spirits there and transform society with the blessings of God's kingdom. One of the results of what God showed me was my book *The Seven Mountain Prophecy*.

The book you are reading now is a follow-up to that earlier book. I had an experience with the Lord in December 2008 in which He spoke to me and said that we had entered into a unique seven-year period of plenty, a time when God's "Josephs" will rise up on the mountains of society. I believe we are in a remarkable season in which God is going after the nations of the world in an unprecedented way.

This book is a book of hope and vision. That's the spirit in which the Lord spoke to me. It does not ignore current and upcoming societal challenges—I realize that the world is being shaken and that the Bible prophesies times of turmoil—but it focuses on the solutions to the world's problems that God will be raising up through His present-day Josephs. God is not afraid of the times ahead; He relishes the opportunity to show who He is. His people do not need to be afraid, either. God invites us to join Him in the amazing work He will do in these exciting times. I will use the biblical story of Joseph as a prophetic parable for the times we are living in and what God is about to do. As God did with Joseph in Egypt, He will be raising up a people who are called not just to save their own necks but to save society itself.

Though the central message in this book is based on a certain time frame, it contains principles that are good for the ages. I believe that in the three-year period of 2008–2011, an entire Joseph people will begin to be positioned to exert unprecedented influence in society. This three-year period may be disconcerting for the very ones God will be preparing to raise up; many will be disconnected from their present missions and assumed assignments and be led to the mountains where they are called to shine. From 2012 on, we will see these Josephs being positioned in a most amazing and supernatural manner as the kingdom of God begins to rest on His sons and daughters who see what He is doing. A small percentage of Josephs are already being positioned, but most will be accelerated through some unique processes in order to be able to shine as they are meant to. Regardless of where you are in that process—and regardless of whether or not you are reading this in the specific seven-year period—this book will help you find and fulfill your destiny as a Joseph of God.

It may help to have read *The Seven Mountain Prophecy* before you read this, but I believe the message in this book can effectively stand on its own. It will release burning hope into those who can hear and see Papa speaking of our future possibilities. His dreams in you will begin to explode as you allow yourself to dare to believe Him for the amazing manifestation of His glory through His sons and daughters. I pray your hearts will be encouraged with the same encouragement I received from the Lord as He spoke these things to me.

Part I

Becoming a Joseph

1

The Joseph Years Begin

S EPTEMBER 29, 2008, began a remarkable new era in human history. At first glance, this day may have seemed significant only to those who live by the Jewish calendar and to those who are keenly interested in the economy, but it was really a landmark day for all of us. It was Rosh Hashanah, the first day of the Hebrew new year, and the stock market dropped a record 777.7 points. Thus began what I call "the Joseph years," when God began intervening in human affairs at a whole new level, and civilization and culture will never be the same again.

A lot of people view that day—and the economic troubles that followed it—as a disaster. I had a vision in which God revealed to me that it was He and not the devil who initiated this rocking of the world's economic institutions. This was an intervention of grace, not the crisis most people have thought it was. The economy had already shown signs of trouble before that day, but the key concern had been narrowly focused on the price of oil and how virtually all experts were projecting sky-high prices for all the foreseeable future. With the rapidly expanding Chinese economy and India's increasing consumption, it seemed that nothing could slow the world's growing demand for oil. The resulting global economic upheaval was already widely felt, creating an economic forecast of doom and gloom. High oil prices were going to be a serious threat to the financial outlook of the entire world. It seemed that this unavoidable fate would impact every nation.

Meanwhile, the U.S. dollar was significantly weakening. Many were discussing whether the new dominant currency ought to be the Euro instead. From a U.S. perspective, these were two barrels of a gun pointing at our financial heart: rising oil prices and a weakening dollar. Our continued dominance as the world's leading economic power was being threatened. But something happened on September 29, 2008.

As the Lord began to show me the implications of the 777.7-point drop in the Dow Jones Industrial Average, I began to see that this was in intervention of His grace on our nation, on other nations, and upon the church in general. I began to understand that the world's economy had heated up so much and was going so fast that it was uncontrollably headed toward a precipice of dreadful consequences. If God had not pulled the plug on our economy, the crash we were headed for would have caused our actual economic hardships to pale in comparison. The slowdown we've experienced certainly brings its own troubles, but we will one day see the grace and mercy of going through a slowdown rather than a total crash.

A PROPHETIC WARNING

I recently shared with our church a prophetic word I had received back in May 1996. I had not previously shared this word publicly for two reasons. One, I didn't really have an audience at that time, as we didn't start our church until 1998. And two, I wasn't sure I believed the word I'd written down. But now it makes sense. Here are some excerpts:

> There will be an end to the pampering and spoiling of ourselves [American Christians]. I see us as a nation facing a financial cliff shortly after the middle of the next decade. My impression is that this will be 2007. I sense that ears will be calloused from being warned of economic "earthquakes" and other financial collapses. I fear that we've become used to hearing "wolf, wolf," and no wolf has shown up.
>
> I share this as a prophetic picture, not from the standpoint of an economist. But I think most of us have seen or read enough to perceive that our national economy seems unhealthy and precarious and headed in the wrong direction. It has survived so long, however, that it's difficult to see exactly what might send it over the edge. I don't know. But I must warn that I see it coming. I see the economic cliff as being very severe, something of historically

significant proportions. I don't see it as Armageddon or the Great Tribulation. It is God taking on the spirit of Mammon because of His great mercy toward us. It will be a time of weeping, wailing, and despair for those who worship Mammon, but a time of great rejoicing for all who love to see the Lord exalted. It will be a time for real Christians to shine and for tares to be exposed. Everyone who calls Him Lord will either know Him as Lord or suffer as one of the ungodly. For those who follow the Lord, there will be a place called "The Provision of the Lord," which will be their rest. But for those who actually bow to Mammon while professing allegiance to the Lord, it will be a very difficult time—but still an opportunity for an improved relationship with the Lord.

Overall, the church is grossly infected with the influence of Mammon. It is safe to assume that almost *all* American believers are unhealthily affected by Mammon's influence in our lives. If we don't learn to subjugate the voice of Mammon, the voice of the Lord will reap the consequences of our idolatry. Even our money-saving strategies will be of no value. Our best strategy must be to develop a relationship of trust with our Creator, and if we don't have that yet, He is giving us a few years to establish that.

I believe the Lord is confirming more and more that we need to invest in relationships. Our culture has taught us "Lone Rangerism"—capitalism, the American Dream, and me, myself, and I—and these attitudes permeate the church. The Lord isn't just wanting us closer to Him; He wants us closer to each other. He will require us to be a Christian community of love in order to survive and even thrive in what's coming.…Religious organizations are going to crash and burn in unprecedented numbers as the Lord cleanses His church. That which represents the *organism* of the church—living stones—will survive and thrive. That which represents *organization* alone—white sepulchers—will dry up and rot.

To summarize what I see happening, the Lord has targeted the ruling spirits of Mammon and Religion. In taking them out, He will cause our natural lives to be turned upside down. Because Mammon and Religion have so infiltrated our spiritual lives, we can expect to be turned upside down, too. This is not a "tragedy" that we can pray against and avoid. It is the work of God to take back control. The more intercession, renewal, and revival that take place, the more certain severe events are likely to take place. Just as the removal of a deadly tumor is severe, painful, and even life-threatening, it is the solution the patient needs. So, severe events the Lord *will* bring.

This word from years ago has suddenly been made manifest. Just this week as I am writing this, renowned economic expert and billionaire Warren Buffett said of current economic realities that it's like we fell off a cliff. As I wrote in 1996, this financial cliff will be "God taking on the spirit of Mammon because of His great mercy toward us." It will not be the end of days but part of the Lord's corrective process specifically designed to upgrade the relationship we, His children, have with Him. This really is an intervention of His grace in order to disconnect His church in spirit from the systems of this world. According to Scripture, those systems are guaranteed to collapse by the very kingdom we are praying in and activating. We have to be shaken and removed from the systems that are being displaced.

> [His] voice then shook the earth; but now He has promised, saying, "Yet once more I shake not only the earth, but also heaven." Now this, "Yet once more," indicates the removal of those things that are being shaken, as of things that are made, that the things which cannot be shaken may remain. Therefore, since we are receiving a kingdom which cannot be shaken, let us have grace, by which we may serve God acceptably with reverence and godly fear. For our God is a consuming fire.
>
> —Hebrews 12:26–29

I believe the Lord initiated a shaking of a removable system and kingdom on September 29, 2008. To the degree we have been "in bed" with that kingdom, we have found ourselves rattled and shaken. Bank accounts, 401(k) plans, and trust funds cannot be our source of confidence for our retirement days. They are "false trust" funds. Only Jehovah-jireh, "the Lord our Provision," has financial security built into His name. It's time to stop leaning on mutual trust funds and lean on Most High trust funds. That's the central instruction of Matthew 6:19–21:

> Do not lay up for yourselves treasures on earth, where moth and rust destroy and where thieves break in and steal; but lay up for yourselves treasures in heaven, where neither moth nor rust destroys and where thieves do not break in and steal. For where your treasure is, there your heart will be also.

Your heart will follow your treasure. Recent economic conditions have revealed that many of us have invested our hearts on earth, where thieves—like greedy practices and Ponzi schemes—have broken in and stolen our treasures. Any money we count on in this realm has a great potential of being lost; that's a guarantee. Christians have recently lost billions or even trillions of dollars that could have greatly advanced God's kingdom on earth. Why? Because many of God's people deceived themselves into thinking that they were reservoirs of finances instead of channels.

Many of us have laid up treasures on earth and covered ourselves with some pseudo-spiritual logic of stewardship, but we haven't fooled the Lord. He sees how our hearts have followed our treasure, and He is after our hearts to get them back. That doesn't mean that all long-term holdings are wrong, of course, but we have kept back more than we should have. The crisis in the American economy is an indictment of wealthy believers in our country. We have wrongfully hoarded in a way that defies reasonable stewardship. Our bank accounts have been deep enough to keep us from leaning on the Lord's accounts. This is a testimony against us.

One of God's greatest pleasures is to provide supernaturally for His children, and He is about to raise up a people who will allow Him this joy. They will be like Joseph, who handled a limitless supply of resources without ever having a personal reservoir. In coming years, real wealth will be released to "Joseph people." But Josephs—both men and women who have a similar role and function in a similar spirit as the biblical Joseph—understand that they are channels, not reservoirs. They manage huge amounts of God's wealth without hoarding it. They fit Jesus' description of the right attitude we should have toward our own needs:

Therefore do not worry, saying, "What shall we eat?" or "What shall we drink?" or "What shall we wear?" For after all these things the Gentiles seek. For your heavenly Father knows that you need all these things. But seek first the kingdom of God and His righteousness, and all these things shall be added to you.

—MATTHEW 6:31–33

We can fool our pastors, our spouses, our associates, and even ourselves about where our heart is and whether we have sought the interests of the kingdom of God *first*. That's because paying Him off as some kind of mafia boss with our tithe doesn't look much different outwardly than being stretched into a true, trusting relationship with Him in which we see Him as our Source. But God knows the truth. If you didn't know where your heart was before the economic crisis, you probably recently found out. As God rescues our economy, don't fall back into the same error. The next time will be much more costly.

A PROPHETIC HOPE

Newspaper headlines on January 16, 2009, quoting the governor of New York, proclaimed a "miracle on the Hudson." A day earlier, U.S. Airways flight 1549 landed in the Hudson River with 153 passengers and two pilots on board. A flock of geese had flown into the plane's engines, but pilot Chesley Sullenberger responded to the crisis quickly and brilliantly by steering the plane into the water and avoiding a fatal crash. What could have been a disaster was widely recognized by the world as a miracle.

Events like these often function as prophetic pictures full of symbolism of what God is saying to His people. What looks like a random event often carries a message for us if we open our eyes and ears and discern His voice. I believe the miracle on the Hudson was one of those events—a powerful statement of God's plans for us. It gives us a picture of hope.

This picture of flight 1549 goes well with the prophetic word I received in 1996. The flock of geese represents the intercession of believers—those who "honk" in heavenly places asking God for intervention. The U.S. Airways plane represents the United States. The location of the flight's crash, very near Wall Street, points to our economy. And Captain Sullenberger's name is significant: *sullen* means "depressed and recessed," and *berger* means "shepherd" in French.

Here's the prophetic picture: the devil wanted our economy to crash by building up its speed. He wanted a plane to crash into New York's tall buildings again—which could have easily happened with a less experienced pilot—just like the last time he tried to destroy our economy. The enemy knows that if he brings down the U.S. economy, the whole world suffers. But God's crash is from His grace. He has allowed our economy to make an emergency landing in response to the prayers of intercessors. The airplane had to fly very low and slow, and after landing on water, it needed the help of emergency rescuers. The Lord is shepherding us through a recession so that all passengers can come out safely. Just as passengers lined the floating wings of the airplane awaiting rescue, so will the Lord rescue us on eagle's wings. He is not finished with America as a superpower; He is correcting us, while simultaneously positioning us to be an even greater blessing to the nations of the world in the future. Our recovery will help rescue 153 nations that were headed toward a catastrophic crash.

I believe this picture may also speak of 153 "sheep nations" in the future. In John 21:1–11, Jesus told Peter and some other disciples to cast their nets on the right side of the boat, and the result was a net full of 153 fish. I'll explain later why I believe this may refer to nations that will turn to the Lord, but I believe at the very least that the Lord gave us this prophetic story in our headlines to reveal His ways in this economic slowdown and "grace" crash. As a result, I believe nations will come to Him with the help of a revived U.S. society and economy.

As a side note, a friend of mine pointed out that the crashed plane was taken to Weeks Marina to be examined. *Weeks* is a word that means "sevens" in the Bible. That number goes well with this book and with the historic stock market day of the 777.7-drop in the Dow Jones average. It's another reminder that God's sevens are now in play, the significance of which we will continue to explore. A new era is coming upon us.

2

Israel Loved Joseph More Than
All of His Sons

HERE IS ONE man in the Bible who has four sevens associated with his life story: Joseph. It begins with the romance between his father and mother. His father, Jacob (a.k.a. Israel), had to serve Rachel's father for two seven-year periods in order to marry her. He had agreed to one term, but after the first seven years, he was given Rachel's older sister, Leah, by deception. He was allowed to marry Rachel a week later, but only after he agreed to serve her father for another seven years. Joseph was the firstborn of the love relationship between Jacob and Rachel, which was quite different than the relationship Jacob had with his other wives.

When this son was thirty years old, he faced two seven-year periods of his own. Because Joseph was able to interpret Pharaoh's dreams, he governed Egypt during seven years of plenty and then seven years of famine. That's why I don't believe it's a coincidence that the U.S. stock market dropped 777.7 on the first day of the Hebrew calendar in a year when our economy crashed. We are to give attention to all four sevens in Joseph's life and what they represented because they contain a message for us today in parable form.

Please understand that I don't believe this is the primary, original meaning of the Joseph story in the Book of Genesis. An interpretation of Scripture that sees "prophetic parables" in biblical stories almost always draws complaints from literalists who charge that the passage is being taken out of context. But while understanding Scripture in context is vitally important, that isn't the *only* value Scripture has. Longstanding Jewish tradition accepts at least four methods of biblical interpretation: the *p'shat* (the literal meaning of a text); the *remez* (the deeper meaning of the text, often only hinted at); the *drash* or *midrash* (the allegorical or metaphorical meaning); and the *sot* (the hidden, mystical meaning). Only the *p'shat* depends entirely on the literal context of the passage, but the other kinds of interpretation have been well accepted throughout history. Even New Testament writers like Matthew, John, and Paul—inspired by the Holy Spirit when they wrote—handled Old Testament passages in some of these ways. It's OK to find hidden meanings in the biblical text; God has enough creativity to inspire a Scripture with multiple layers in it.

A lack of understanding of Hebraic interpretation has caused many Greek-minded seminarians and scholars to miss many of the treasures hidden for us in God's Word. Ephesians 3:10 speaks of the "manifold wisdom of God"—i.e., His "many-sided" or "many-faceted" wisdom. What follows is an interpretation of the Joseph story that extracts some of His wisdom, imbedded in the text for us to find today.

DOES GOD HAVE FAVORITES?

Now Jacob dwelt in the land where his father was a stranger, in the land of Canaan. This is the history of Jacob. Joseph, being seventeen years old, was feeding the flock with his brothers. And the lad was with the sons of Bilhah and the sons of Zilpah, his father's wives; and Joseph brought a bad report of them to his father. Now Israel loved Joseph more than all his children, because he was the son of his old age. Also he made him a tunic of many colors.

—GENESIS 37:1–3

These three verses begin the interesting story of Joseph and how he rose to power over all the land of Egypt. We will follow him as he goes from being a sheep herder to being sold to Midianite merchants, to being sold to Potiphar, to being sent to Pharaoh's prison, and then standing before Pharaoh himself, when he was suddenly thrust into the very position he had dreamed of since he was very young. This is exactly the kind of journey God requires of all who would be willing to be Josephs in this momentous time of history.

The key phrase I want to focus on in this passage is "Now Israel loved

Joseph more than all his sons" (v. 3). I'm going to suggest from this phrase that God has favorites today, whom He will honor in unique ways. Notice that the passage does not say that Israel didn't love Joseph's brothers. He loved all of his sons. But he loved Joseph more. I believe we are about to see God's favoritism for certain kinds of sons and daughters today.

All Christians are invited to be "Josephs;" there's no favoritism in the invitation itself. But to be a Joseph, there has to be something different about you, something that distinguishes you from a run-of-the-mill believer. The Bible is full of stories of God's favor on certain people who responded to His heart. Though everyone is invited to be His friend, only certain people are called "friends" in Scripture.

We see this with Abraham, for example, who is called a friend of God (2 Chron. 20:7; Isa. 41:8; James 2:23). John called himself "the beloved"—the disciple whom Jesus loved—because of the special affection the Lord showed for him, as when John leaned against Jesus at the Last Supper, for example (John 13:25). Even though God loves everyone, Proverbs 8:17 tells us, "I love those who love me, And those who seek me diligently will find me." Jesus said, "If anyone loves Me, he will keep My word; and My Father will love him, and We will come to him and make Our home with him" (John 14:23). While it's true that God is no respecter of persons (Acts 10:34; Rom. 2:11, KJV), those who diligently seek Him will find more of Him. Since God *is* love, to find more of Him is to find more of His love. Therefore, some are "loved" more than others because of how they have chosen to pursue God. Those who hold back are going to experience less of His love.

ISRAEL'S FAVORITE

Why was Joseph Israel's favorite? For one thing, he was the first child of Rachel, the wife Jacob adored and for whom he had worked for fourteen years. But Genesis 37:3 also tells us that Joseph was "the son of his old age." Israel would actually live for several more decades, but he was old when Joseph was born. That's a significant part of the story that relates to what God is doing today. Isaiah 2:2 speaks of "the latter days" when something unprecedented will happen in the household of God. We have entered a divine *kairos* time when the Lord is raising up a Joseph people ready to step into the things He has hoped for since the beginning of time.

15

Israel already had ten sons, but his eleventh stirred him in an unprecedented way. Leah and the two handmaidens through whom Jacob had borne his previous sons had obviously been fruitful, but Rachel birthed the "love child" he had longed for. This is the child who would grow up to have authority over the nations—a prophetic picture of Revelation 2:26, in which Jesus promises power over nations to those who overcome. The number eleven represents prophecy, and it also speaks of the eleventh-hour ministry rising up in the last times. As we will see, everything about Joseph relates to intimacy and the prophetic. The Joseph people who will arise under his mantle of favor to displace darkness from the mountaintops will be a prophetic people. If we don't get that, we'll remain one of the ten brothers who didn't understand Joseph or his assignment.

Joseph brought "a bad report" of his brothers to his father (Gen. 37:2). Some people think this portrays Joseph as a spoiled brat or a tattletale, but I don't think that's the case. It seems clear that the report was true; the brothers really were doing some bad things. I believe Joseph could see how lackadaisical and visionless his brothers were and that God had already put into him a calling to invade society, to see God move in unprecedented ways, and to make entire nations His inheritance. But these brothers were just doing time—or, to put it in modern terms, just waiting for the Rapture.

We can infer a lot from this story in Scripture. There are parallels for today. A Joseph people is rising up out of the darkness (Isa. 60:1–3), and they can see that their "brothers" don't seem to care that the central fact of the Great Commission is to disciple "all nations" (Matt. 28:17–18). Those who see the full ramifications of the Great Commission have a bad report about our brothers to give to the Father: "Papa, they are just doing time, waiting for You to come rescue them out of the darkness one day. They only care about what's going on in the sheepfold—the mountain of religion within the four walls of the church—and they don't understand that if they don't rise and shine, the darkness of the nations will overtake them." This kind of report only confirms to our Father that we have been hanging out with Him long enough to get His heart for society.

Israel didn't chastise Joseph for his complaint about his brothers, and God doesn't chastise those of us today who want to see society shaken and reformed by His power. The heart of Joseph is the heart of a reformer who operates from a foundation of intimacy with the Lord. In these latter days, we will clearly see that God loves and favors reformers above those who have only a passion to sell the best "death benefits"—a gospel of salvation that focuses entirely on signing the dotted line so that we can have eternal life. The gospel of the kingdom is a lot more comprehensive. It includes salvation, obviously, but it is primarily the good news that in the Last Days, the mountain of the house of the Lord will be established on the tops of the mountains and the nations will run to it in response to its light (Isa. 2:2).

I recently had a vision in which I saw Joseph's coat of many colors and how it applies to us today. In the vision, the Lord called it "the seven mountain mantle." I was shown that only Josephs will carry the authority to displace the enemy and his darkness from the seven mountains of society. The coat of many colors had all the colors of the rainbow, which related to the seven spirits of God (Rev. 5:6) that are sent into all the earth to dispel darkness from the mountains of society—the mountains of government, education, economy/business, media, family, religion, and celebration (arts and enter-tainment). I believe this vision means that God is going to do something unprecedented in the days to come. We really are going to see the fulfillment of Isaiah 2:2—"Now it shall come to pass in the latter days That the mountain of the LORD's house Shall be established on the top of the mountains, And shall be exalted above the hills; And all nations shall flow to it."

God is going to manifest Himself in seven ways; He will showcase Himself in a particular way in each of society's mountains. These seven manifesta-tions won't be about what He does but who He is. He will show seven facets of Himself. For example, He is the God of government, and He manifests Himself as the Prince of Peace. Righteousness and justice are the founda-tions of His throne (Ps. 89:14). In Isaiah 9:7 we read, "Of the increase of His government and peace There will be no end." He will prove to be the God of government and, as we will see, the God of every other sector of society. The rising Josephs in our generation will carry His presence into the seven mountains in the years to come.

3

The Rachel Church and the Leah Church

I N ORDER TO really understand Jacob's special love for Joseph, we have to go back to the beginning of Jacob's love story. Genesis 29 gives us insight into Jacob's (Israel's) relationship with his bride, and I believe that relationship reflects the love of God's heart in a way that's very significant for us today.

Now while he was still speaking with them, Rachel came with her father's sheep, for she was a shepherdess. And it came to pass, when Jacob saw Rachel the daughter of Laban his mother's brother, and the sheep of Laban his mother's brother, that Jacob went near and rolled the stone from the well's mouth, and watered the flock of Laban his mother's brother. Then Jacob kissed Rachel, and lifted up his voice and wept. And Jacob told Rachel that he was her father's relative and that he was Rebekah's son. So she ran and told her father....Now Laban had two daughters: the name of the elder was Leah, and the name of the younger was Rachel. Leah's eyes were delicate, but Rachel was beautiful of form and appearance. Now Jacob loved Rachel; so he said, "I will serve you seven years for Rachel your younger daughter." And Laban said, "It is better that I give her to you than that I should give her to another man. Stay with me." So Jacob served seven years for Rachel, and they seemed only a few days to him because of the love he had for her.

—GENESIS 29:9–12, 16–20

Let's look at this story as a parable, with Rachel and Leah representing two manifestations of the church. There is only one church of Jesus Christ, of course—all true believers of all times and all places—but we can identify two distinct attitudes or manifestations within the church.

"When Jacob Saw Rachel"

Jacob's passionate response to the sight of Rachel is unparalleled in Scripture. He was instantly moved by her and drawn to her. When he saw her, he went near and "rolled the stone from the well's mouth" (Gen. 29:10). In the very next verse, he kissed her and lifted up his voice and wept!

What was it about Rachel that moved Jacob so much? Was it simply her physical beauty? Or was there something more? The passage doesn't spell it out for us, but I think we can make some conjectures based on the scriptural evidence. If we're looking at this romance metaphorically as a relationship between the Lord and His church, then it's possible for us to move the Lord and become irresistible to Him by the beauty of the way we carry ourselves. Throughout Scripture, God is a relational God far more than being a God of principles. As with all relational beings, He is attracted to certain characteristics in people and has to put up with others.

"For She Was a Shepherdess"

Part of Rachel's beauty was in the fact that she was a shepherdess who came to the well with her sheep. There were three other flocks of sheep already gathered around the well, but they were all being tended by men (Gen. 29:4). Rachel was different. She wasn't just sitting home being "normal." She had a mission that extended beyond her home. She had a nurturing, shepherding heart, and she was involved in a wider sphere of influence than just her home. Whoever would win her over would have to know that she had more drive than the average girl.

Jacob was so moved by Rachel that he went near and rolled the stone from the well's mouth. It was a very large stone (Gen. 29:2), and it wasn't yet time for the stone to be removed (v. 8). Yet Jacob was moved to action and helped water all of Rachel's flock, as though he couldn't help quickly enough for this outside-the-box girl. After acting on her behalf, he couldn't restrain his passion for her; it seems that he *had* to kiss her. He was so moved by this kiss of true love that he lifted up his voice in a cry of passion and longing. He didn't just want to do something *for* her; he wanted to do something *with* her. He saw something in her that reflected the type of person he was. He was attracted to her reciprocal DNA. He immediately let Rachel know that he wanted more: marriage, intimacy, and children.

"SO SHE RAN AND TOLD HER FATHER"

Rachel was apparently not just mildly OK with Jacob's forwardness. He may have been the initiator of the kiss, but she let him kiss her. And when she found out he wanted more, she *ran* home to her father, Laban. She was ready to respond to the one she had been waiting for. She wanted more of him. She was moved *by* him, moved *for* him, and moved *to* him. Her interest in Jacob was 100 percent relational. She had not even stopped to ask him about his economic standing or his prospects for the future. She had no idea what was in it for her, other than Jacob himself. The relational spark of passion was so intense that these other matters would just take care of themselves. If she could just be with Jacob, all other things would be added to her.

This was love at first sight by both sides, and both would pursue this matter.

"NOW LABAN HAD TWO DAUGHTERS"

A complication arose for Jacob. He found out that Laban had two daughters. The older one was Leah, and according to tradition she would have to be married first. Jacob was surprised at how Laban held to tradition; when he thought he was marrying Rachel, her father snuck Leah into the deal.

"LEAH'S EYES WERE DELICATE"

While Rachel was "beautiful of form and appearance," all we know of Leah is that she had delicate, or weak, eyes. Rachel was beautiful, nurturing, passionate, and original, but all we know of Leah comes through a comment about her eyes. She represents the part of the church that has little or no vision. She was married to Jacob, but only in a logical, practical, and legal fashion. The relationship between Jacob and Leah functioned by principles rather than by passion. There were sons from their union, but they weren't Jacob's favorite sons. He stuck to his covenant agreement, but neither Leah nor her sons moved Jacob's heart to unusual manifestations of passion and favor. That wasn't his choice; it was theirs. They seemed to look to him more for what he secured for them rather than for who he was. Leah was looking for the normal conveniences of life that her marriage with Jacob would provide. But Rachel was looking for Jacob himself.

It's possible to interpret the "Leah church" as a representation of the Jewish people. They are legally entitled to certain privileges and rights from God because a man named Abraham touched His heart and became His friend. That doesn't mean they are saved apart from Jesus, of course, but they have covenantal blessings coming to them whether they move God's heart or not. They can be passionless and visionless and still be entitled to a form of love. In this context, the "Rachel church" would represent all Jews and Gentiles who come to God through Yeshua (Jesus)—those who are attracted to who Jesus is and come to saving faith because of that. In the fullness of this story line, it is ultimately Rachel's son Joseph who brings salvation to Leah's house, even though she was the one first in covenant with her husband. That's one way to look at this as a parable.

I believe, however, that the greater truth for today is that there is a Rachel church and a Leah church even among those who profess faith in and through Jesus. The Leah church has very weak vision. She knows the Word of God without knowing the God of the Word very well. She reads the Bible, prays for her food, gives tithes and offerings, goes to church on Sundays, knows biblical principles, but generally has a legal relationship with God rather than a relationship of passion and insight. The Leah church is most concerned with "life insurance" and "death benefits." She will even make a significant effort to get others to sign on the dotted line and make sure their death benefits are secure. But she has very little vision for anything else here on earth. She will produce sons, but, like Joseph's ten older brothers, they will have very little sense of destiny. She doesn't understand the Lord's heart for rescuing and discipling entire nations rather than just individuals because she pays more attention to doctrine than to the Lord's voice. She is only trying to decipher what was written at least two thousand years ago and nothing more. Finding God's heart for today and for this world is too difficult and too risky, so she settles for the safe assumptions of the relationship.

The Leah church is looking for the easy way out, and her ears itch for explanations of the End Times that require nothing of the believer but to wait to be rescued. She has no vision and therefore no faith to see God do anything great on earth through her, other than rescue a few souls from hell. Doctrines of the Rapture are very convenient to her, and she embraces them not because of their biblical foundations but because escaping the world fits well with her weak vision. She cannot imagine a God who is so excited about partnering with a love-mate that He will display His glory and its transforming power through her as a demonstration to the whole world and even the universe. She doesn't understand that He wants the fruit of this relationship to carry His "tunic of many colors" and display His favor even in the highest sectors of society. The Leah church can't imagine God raising up a people who would rescue and reform society itself. She doesn't know His heart for the nations because she doesn't relate to Him that way. She has read that His glory will cover the earth, but she has no vision to believe that this is possible during her lifetime, even though Scripture is clear that His glory will be seen upon us (Isa. 60:1–3). The Leah church is managing to populate the hereafter with many children, but is doing little or nothing for the here and now. She has no grid for understanding Jesus' prayer that His kingdom would come "on earth as it is in heaven" (Matt. 6:10; Luke 11:2). That would be just too wonderful, too ideal, and too impossible. She has delicate and weak eyes.

"But Rachel Was Beautiful"

Jacob volunteered to serve Laban for seven years in order to marry Rachel, "and they seemed only a few days to him because of the love he had for her" (Gen. 29:20). Even now, there's a rising church that has absolutely smitten God's heart. God has recognized a Rachel segment of the church that dares to see Him differently and dares to believe for a greater extension of how far shepherding can go. This Rachel church believes that the entire world is our sheepfold. This is where she meets with her love and where He kisses her. This is where He provides a well of presence and where He displays unusual passion and interest in her. Rachel would never have been content to just sing three songs from a hymnal and take a seat. Likewise, the Rachel church will not even pretend she is meeting with Him unless His presence is there. And once His presence is found, she may go an hour or two—or whatever is necessary—to satisfy the relational longing of her soul. She is not looking to "check off" the legal aspect of their relationship. She will extravagantly pour herself out on Him in every place that He will meet her.

For the Rachel church, it isn't enough for others to tell her what "Jacob" has been saying to others. She must hear something personal. She will seek His voice for something fresh and relevant specifically to her and for her. She will be frustrated until He has personally communicated with her. Some may berate her for believing He still speaks outside of His original letters of courtship, and others may think she is too hungry for "the prophetic;" but His voice is a lifeline to her. She is not in this relationship just for the bene-fits. She must have *Him!* She is relationally driven, and out of this deep level of intimacy, she becomes more aware than anyone else of what's important to Him. She gets to know the One who asks the Father for the nations as an inheritance (Ps. 2:8). She understands what moves Him to weep over a city (Matt. 23:37). She sees both His love and His power, but, more importantly, the power of His love. And because of her love for Him, He won't relent until He has seen heaven come down to earth *on her.* As He makes clear, she is receiving a kingdom that cannot be shaken (Heb. 12:28).

The Bible is clear that Jacob loved Rachel more than Leah. Because of that love, he served Laban for another seven years, making two seven-year periods that were sown into the relationship that would bring forth Joseph. Just as Jacob invested a lot of time and passion into his much-anticipated love child, so does God look forward to the children of his Rachel church—those who will act and look more like Him than anyone other than Jesus ever has.

4

Dreaming the Father's Dreams for Society

Now Joseph had a dream, and he told it to his brothers; and they hated him even more. So he said to them, "Please hear this dream which I have dreamed: There we were, binding sheaves in the field. Then behold, my sheaf arose and also stood upright; and indeed your sheaves stood all around and bowed down to my sheaf."

—GENESIS 37:5–7

THIS DREAM IS very interesting when we take a close look at it. Because Joseph is filled with the DNA of a divine romance, his dreams are simply reflective of who he is. His great "arrogance," as some people call it, was that his sheaf "arose and also stood upright" (Gen. 37:7). Leah's sons had no vision, so they did not stand at the stature they were supposed to. Joseph just inherently knew that he was to "stand upright." He didn't impose dominion on his brothers; he just arose and stood up to the height he was supposed to be.

Romans 8:21 says that "the creation itself also will be delivered from the bondage of corruption into the glorious liberty of the children of God." Some kind of "standing up" of the children of God must take place in the last days. Creation groans and travails in looking for that. Creation will not be delivered from its bondage of corruption in the context of some separate millennium. What creation is waiting for is not the return of Jesus but the standing up of Josephs—the sons and daughters of destiny. This idea is foreign to Leah's sons because they are a product of weak vision and are therefore indignant.

> And his brothers said to him, "Shall you indeed reign over us? Or shall you indeed have dominion over us?" So they hated him even more for his dreams and for his words.
>
> —GENESIS 37:8

Joseph was beginning to dream the Father's dreams. The goal is reigning and having dominion. We know from Genesis that these are God's original dreams: "Then God said, 'Let Us make man in Our image, according to Our likeness; let them have dominion'" (Gen. 1:26).

What do we mean by *dominion*? A lot of people confuse the word with *domination*, but that isn't what we're talking about at all. The assignment in the Garden of Eden was to fill the earth and subdue it—to bring it under the Lord's governance through His people. When we talk about dominion today, we aren't thinking of dominating people but of ruling over the enemy. Our role as children of God is not to become lords over people but to deliver society from darkness. We bring light, not dominance. Jesus came to overcome the enemy's work through His people: "For this purpose the Son of God was manifested, that He might destroy the works of the devil" (1 John 3:8). When the triune God reproduces man in *Their* image and *Their* likeness, the result is a Joseph, someone who carries His purposes into the nations of the world and brings His light into the kingdoms of earth. To intrinsically know that dominion over darkness is our basic inheritance is proof that we carry God's image and His likeness.

The Son of God did not come just to rescue souls from the talons of the devil. He came to destroy the devil's works—his works in government, in the media, in educational institutions, in Hollywood, in Wall Street, in families, and in the religious landscape. Until this flows naturally from our spiritual DNA, we are the spiritual equivalent of Jacob's first ten sons. Anywhere we don't bring light will remain in darkness, and in order to bring light, we must arise and stand upright. Only those who come from Leah could consider something so close to God's heart to be heresy.

Joseph Keeps Dreaming

> Then he dreamed still another dream and told it to his brothers,
> and said, "Look, I have dreamed another dream. And this time,
> the sun, the moon, and the eleven stars bowed down to me."
> —Genesis 37:9

Yet again Joseph was dreaming of ruling, reigning, and dominion. He may have had some youthful zeal and may have lacked wisdom, but he knew he had seen into the future. The sun and the moon were his parents and the eleven stars were his eleven brothers (younger brother Benjamin included). What he lacked in wisdom he knew by spiritual insight. They were living in a dark time, and they were called to shine.

Again, we see this clearly in Isaiah 60:1–3:

> Arise, shine; for your light has come! And the glory of the Lord
> is risen upon you. For behold, the darkness shall cover the earth,
> and deep darkness the people; but the Lord will arise over you,
> and His glory will be seen upon you. The Gentiles shall come to
> your light, and kings to the brightness of your rising.

If we apply Joseph's situation to today, we could say that Joseph had seen a dark day upon the face of the earth, but the solution he foresaw was not hoping for a "Rapture" to save them but them being stars that shine in the darkness. Stars are always there, but no one notices them until it's nighttime. Joseph knew his brothers were also called to be stars in the night—the Joseph invitation is for all God's children. But Joseph also knew that his brothers had no prophetic vision to see this, and therefore they would bow to him.

Many people know the Word of God and realize that He is offering the gift of salvation to all. But you have to know the God of the Word in order to realize we can also eradicate darkness to such a point that entire nations can function by the light of our arising into true sonship. In the first case, you know the principled benefits of the legal covenant; but in the second, you know the relational benefits that spring from the overflow of His heart.

GOD'S DREAMS INITIATE GOD'S PROCESS

When Joseph declared his dreams, a process began to unfold in his life. The very dreams of God released the process that would prepare him for the ruling and reigning that he was dreaming. To put it in terms of the metaphor we've been making out of his life, he had dreamed of being beyond the "four walls" of the flock and affecting society itself. Joseph was about to connect with the means to make him ready for the dominion he would eventually exert.

Psalms 105 retells some of Israel's history and then makes a particular statement about Joseph:

> *Until the time that his word came to pass, the word of the* LORD *tested him.* The king sent and released him, the ruler of the people let him go free. He made him lord of his house, and ruler of all his possessions.
>
> —PSALM 105:19–21, EMPHASIS ADDED

Joseph's dream was credited to him as a word from God, and the very word he received created the tests that would prepare him to survive the awesome weight of his destiny. He was called to deliver a society out of darkness, but he would have to lean on his intimacy with the Lord to get there. This is an enormously significant truth for those of us today who are dreaming Joseph's dreams for society. The prophetic vision or faith is enough to get you started up the mountains, but it will only be the great grace of perseverance and endurance that will ultimately secure the destiny we've dreamed about.

5

Hated by Leah's Sons

THE FIRST PART of Joseph's process was a painful one. His brothers hated him for what he had dreamed. This is something we face in our mission, too. Our proper response to this reality is important, as the very ones that hate us are the ones we are called to deliver. We can learn a lot from looking at the passages about the ten brothers' reactions.

> When his brothers saw that their father loved him more than all his brothers, they hated him and could not speak peaceably to him.
>
> —GENESIS 37:4

The coat of many colors is what first stirred the hatred of Joseph's brothers. They might have suspected for some time that he was the favorite son, but when Israel made it obvious by making Joseph a coat of many colors, it released so much hatred in them that they could not even speak peaceably to him. They were really wanting to resent Israel, but it was hard to be mad at Israel, just as it's hard for us to be mad at God, so they spewed all their hatred out on Joseph. To draw a parallel for today, this shows up as some sectors of the church bashing and railing against those who step into the supernatural dimension of God's favor while ignoring the fact that God is the one who has placed His favor on these people. Anger is directed at God's people for something God has clearly done.

Joseph's brothers had two options. They could either ask themselves why they weren't getting a multi-colored coat and pursue the relational path of obtaining it, or they could pretend that Joseph's favor was counterfeit or a heresy. When Josephs are supernaturally invading society and bringing God's light to the nations, it testifies against the virtual fruitlessness of those who see the Rapture as the only source of hope for societal ills. They must either come to terms with their own barrenness or conspire together to defame and discredit the Josephs. If Josephs are stigmatized, then passive, defeatist eschatology can still provide excuses for living a life far below God's standards. The choice is to live as a bowed sheaf rather than an upright sheaf.

> Now Joseph had a dream, and he told it to his brothers; and they hated him even more....So they hated him even more for his dreams and for his words....And his brothers envied him, but his father kept the matter in mind.
>
> —GENESIS 37:5, 8, 11

The last verse may be the most revealing. The brothers were actually envious. They knew Joseph was closer to Papa. He was getting a many-colored coat, and they weren't. They knew Joseph was getting prophetic dreams and that they weren't. Their lack of supernatural inheritance led them to hate and envy. They never discerned that their apparent lack of favor was not initiated by Papa. The sons of Leah and the maids were limited by their own assumptions, just as the Leah church today is limited by its own doctrinal restrictions. Their own weak vision kept them out of a circle of experiential love and favor that Papa would have loved to bestow upon them all.

Today, "Leah's sons" have embraced a defeatist eschatology that magnifies the Antichrist, the false prophet, the beast, and every other dire prophecy of Tribulation. This doctrinal approach has a convenient escape clause that takes us completely out of the great darkness—even as more than 250,000 believers are martyred for their faith every year. In this eschatology of an early or immediate Rapture, there's no place for Josephs to arise because everything is destined for disaster anyway. It's a visionless view of the latter days, and it can't make any sense of God's offer to Jesus to ask for the nations as an inheritance (Ps. 2:8). If all evil people have been destroyed and all righteous people have been raptured, that would leave Jesus with a bare planet to inherit. Instead, we're told not that we will check out one day but that "the creation eagerly waits for the revealing of the sons of God" (Rom. 8:19).

"Joseph's brothers" hate us because we believe this kind of "heresy." How dare we believe that creation is actually waiting for sons of God to arise and stand upright? The brothers' erroneous doctrine proceeds from their own loss of true identity. They don't see that Jesus is gaga over His bride and that He wants to showcase her on every mountaintop. They don't see that He loves divine partnership and relational dynamics. They don't see a God who is giddy to prove to every power and principality that turned against Him that love never fails. Satan boasts against God that even though He can rescue souls, He can't really see His kingdom come to earth through those who claim to love Him. But before it's all over, God will raise up a Joseph people. And through them, He will showcase the lovers of God at the tops of the mountains of society.

LEAH'S SONS WILL ONE DAY SEE

"And behold your eyes…see that it is my mouth that speaks to you. So you shall tell my father of all my glory in Egypt, and of all that you have seen"….Moreover he kissed all his brothers and wept over them, and after that his brothers talked with him.

—GENESIS 45:12–13, 15

Joseph people must always remember that even when brothers act like enemies, they are not. They are still brothers who either here or in heaven will one day lose their weakness of vision and see. The brothers' hostility, though bad for them initially, is part of the very process that will prepare Joseph—the Joseph of Genesis and the Josephs of today—to rule in society. As we will see, this is the initial catalyst for propelling a Joseph up the mountains of society. He will be forced out of traditional church life into seeing and receiving the unshakeable kingdom. What his brothers mean for evil, God means for good.

6

Thrust into the Marketplace

JOSEPH'S BROTHERS CONSPIRED to kill him, but after stripping him of his coat of many colors, they settled for selling him into slavery. Though the physical coat had been stripped from him, he had already received the mantle of favor.

> Then Midianite traders passed by; so the brothers pulled Joseph up and lifted him out of the pit, and sold him to the Ishmaelites for twenty shekels of silver. And they took Joseph to Egypt
> —GENESIS 37:28

The Joseph of Genesis, who had only been dreaming God's dreams of further influence, was now forcibly thrust onto the mountains of society. If Egypt represents society in this story, and I believe it does, Joseph reached four different stages of influence over his culture: the Midianite trader stage, the Potiphar's house stage, the Pharaoh's prison stage, and the ruler of the land stage.

OUTSIDE THE FOUR WALLS

About ten to fifteen years ago, a renewed marketplace vision arose from the church with scores of books coming out on the subject. What was unique about this new focus and what set it apart from other previous focuses of faith in the marketplace is that it was accompanied by faith that society could be transformed. This movement has been a preliminary manifestation of the Joseph company that will soon be shining on every mountain of society. It went beyond the goal of just getting people saved and of having prayer meetings. The stated mission in several books on this topic was to see societal transformation. Though the movement lacked a template for how this could viably take place, there was faith to declare that transformation was possible. A primary goal of this emphasis was to see the 97 percent of believers who will never serve as church staff do something in their nine-to-five life as their ministry. This movement still exists, and its pioneering focus has been very helpful for where God wants to take us. I believe we will one day look back on it as the Midianite trader stage of the rising Josephs—a time when God's beloved people are taken into the world to manifest God's glory.

God calls us to be leaders in society.

> The LORD will make you the head and not the tail; you shall be
> above only, and not be beneath, if you heed the commandments
> of the LORD your God.
>
> —DEUTERONOMY 28:13

We were not designed to react to everything the enemy does in the mountains of society, as is often our pattern, but to be proactive and force the enemy to react to us. We have generally found ourselves being the tail of society because we have lived almost exclusively on the mountain of religion. Our lack of vision regarding our inheritance has prevented us from being the head.

Joseph, too, started his journey to destiny as a member of the tail. That's where his brothers and the rest of the family had lived. It was what they were used to. Just by dreaming God's dreams for his life, Joseph prophetically activated the circumstances that would bring about his destiny.

This is similar to some amazing recent discoveries in the subatomic quantum world. Scientists are baffled by how "unseen" particles and waves become activated and visible simply by being observed. In the quantum world all matter is connected, so activation in one place brings responses and ramifications in other places. In the world of faith, your destiny gets activated the moment you prophetically see it. Joseph's dreams caused him to observe his unseen destiny, which then released a process into his life. This process was designed so that if he submitted to it, he would be prepared to bear sustainable fruit in his place of destiny and not be picked off the mountains, as others are. The process itself would help him develop the spiritual strength he would need to carry the weight of his calling. In fact, that wouldn't be a bad quote to put on your refrigerator: "Your process is designed to develop the muscles you will need to sustain the weight of your destiny." For Joseph, step one of the process was shining among Midianite traders.

The Hebrew word for *Midianite* means "strife, striving, and stress." Many of us know the reality of this condition, especially those who operate on the mountain of business/economy, which is illegally being run by a spirit of Mammon. Joseph carried two essential qualities required of anyone who would be successful in climbing this mountain: intimacy with God and a prophetic anointing. The first quality makes the second one work. The evidence that you are spending time with God is that He speaks to you. "My sheep hear My voice," Jesus said (John 10:27).

Joseph was a product of true love, and his relational strength in God would sustain and promote him throughout the process toward his destiny. He also carried the favor and authority of the "seven mountain mantle" given to him by his father. We've seen his many-colored coat as a sign of his father's favor and authority, and if we have our Father's favor and authority, we will be able to displace the darkness in society. Wearing this mantle doesn't mean we're a big deal, but it does mean that God is a big deal. From the enemy's standpoint, it makes us dangerous because God had enough confidence or hope in us to put it on us.

We aren't told how long or how well Joseph served the Midianite traders, but it must have been well enough for them to realize that he was valuable property. Genesis 37 ends with a sentence that seems to report nothing more than a simple fact, but it's really a strong statement of Joseph's favor: "Now the Midianites had sold him in Egypt to Potiphar, an officer of Pharaoh and captain of the guard" (Gen. 37:36). His captors must have been singing his praises to some degree to get an officer of Pharaoh like Potiphar to buy him. Joseph had fulfilled the first stage of his process well.

7

Up the Mountain into Potiphar's House

THE MOMENT JOSEPH'S process began, every subsequent shift of his life was a promotion. Those shifts certainly didn't look like promotions. Joseph probably couldn't recognize them as such at the time, but every stage of process brought him higher up the mountain. Every stage took him closer to being the head rather than the tail and to realizing the fulfillment of what he had seen in his dreams. Only in hindsight would that become obvious, but let's remember that as we follow Joseph up the mountain of societal influence. His call was no longer just looking for "decisions for Christ," so to speak; his mission went far beyond that. He was on his way to reforming society. If he didn't get to his place of destiny, civilization itself may have ceased to exist as it had.

The next two stages of Joseph's pilgrimage into destiny are found in Genesis 39, a passage we'll focus on in this chapter and the next.

> Now Joseph had been taken down to Egypt. And Potiphar, an officer of Pharaoh, captain of the guard, an Egyptian, bought him from the Ishmaelites who had taken him down there. The LORD was with Joseph, and he was a successful man; and he was in the house of his master the Egyptian. And his master saw that the LORD was with him and that the LORD made all he did to prosper in his hand.
>
> —GENESIS 39:1–3

More accolades for Joseph will come, but first let's stop and look at some key issues.

"THE LORD WAS WITH JOSEPH"

The first comment on his success is that "the Lord is with him" (Gen. 39:3). We'll see this phrase again in Joseph's story, and it highlights the fact that intimacy with God is the starting point from which everything else must flow. If that isn't the foundation of our lives, we may just be children of Leah. The reason the Lord was with Joseph was because Joseph was with the Lord. He was already close to Him, but now circumstances had eliminated any other support structure. A Joseph ultimately cannot fail if closeness with the Lord remains the testimony of his or her life.

"AND HE WAS A SUCCESSFUL MAN"

Before you can be a successful businessperson, a successful politician, a successful musician, or a successful anything, you must be a successful man or woman. As we view the ongoing developments of Joseph's life, it becomes evident that he was an excellent administrator. He seems to have been specifically gifted for that, even without ever having studied administration. His very close walk with the Lord caused him to manifest great stewardship in all areas of his life, a characteristic that causes someone to appear very administratively gifted.

The best gifts are those that flow from a profound relationship with God. Out of that kind of intimate relationship, you learn how to prioritize matters with uncanny wisdom. True administrative gifts must come with a significant element of wisdom, which in its purest form comes straight from the Holy Spirit. When that is coupled with a prophetic gifting, the result is an unparalleled ability to administrate. We can probably assume that Joseph's dreaming did not stop, and that through the interpretation of these dreams he was able to untangle many knots that daily presented themselves to him. In simple terms, then, hearing God and obeying God are the two requisites for being successful.

"And His Master Saw That God Was with Him"

Not only was God with Joseph, but society itself recognized that God was with him. When you are the firstborn of Rachel, you operate in another level of reliance on God. Reliance on God is the highest form of spiritual maturity and the greatest evidence of intimacy with Him. Joseph had moved higher up the mountain without leaning on his education and training. He was leaning on the Lord.

This is usually the hardest thing for trained and educated people to do when they climb the mountains of society. Training and education are generally necessary, but they usually only come with a humanistic level of wisdom-potential that's available even to those without Christ. People around us will know God is with us when they recognize that the gifts we're accessing are beyond the instruction we've received from education. We may use the knowledge we've gained from human instruction, but we lean on the One who is the air we breathe. We operate out of His resources.

As we continue to look at Joseph's life, we discover more keys for being a mountain climber.

> So Joseph found favor in his sight, and served him. Then he made
> him overseer of his house, and all that he had he put under his
> authority. So it was, from the time that he had made him over-
> seer of his house and all that he had, that the LORD blessed the
> Egyptian's house for Joseph's sake; and the blessing of the LORD
> was on all that he had in the house and in the field. Thus he left
> all that he had in Joseph's hand, and he did not know what he
> had except for the bread which he ate. Now Joseph was hand-
> some in form and appearance.
>
> —GENESIS 39:4–6

This is an amazingly detailed picture of what favor looks like. Potiphar put everything in his household under Joseph and worried about nothing other than the bread he ate. Joseph was made overseer over everything because his administrative gift was a supernatural gift.

"THE LORD BLESSED THE EGYPTIAN'S HOUSE FOR JOSEPH'S SAKE"

We have to understand this part of our Lord. In the minds of many people, all kingdom activity is summed up in the issue of whether anyone got saved or healed. But kingdom activity in Joseph's story looked a lot different. His household—and, in the metaphor we've been using, society as a whole—was blessed because of him. The goal of Joseph's ministry wasn't to get Potiphar "saved." God offers the gift of salvation to everyone, but He does have other aspects of Himself He wants to showcase. Through Joseph, God ultimately blessed those who didn't know Him because they recognized the gift of God that was in Joseph.

Joseph himself would not gain any financial blessing from this season of his life, but both he and God were fine with that. Are you OK with being a blessing for others without having any of the blessing directly splash back to you? This is another part of the Joseph Test. You do things as though you are doing them for the Lord, and you let Him worry about the details. As we will continue to see, Joseph never had to strategize how to get to the mountaintop he had dreamed of. He never resorted to striving and manipulating, as someone who did not rely on God would do. Instead, his focus was (1) being with God and (2) being a successful man. The same God who made the prophetic promise of his destiny could get him there if those two priorities were in order.

So far in his life, Joseph had not seemed to personally benefit from his gifts. His brothers made money selling him to the Midianites. The Midianites probably made out substantially better by selling him to Potiphar. Potiphar was blessed "in the house" and "in the field" because of Joseph. Through human eyes, Joseph seemed to be no closer to his destiny. Were people really going to bow down to him? He wasn't even a free man yet. He was still a prisoner of the nine-to-five life. He didn't own his own business. But in God, most logical progression happens only in hindsight. In other words, only after the fact does it become evident where and how the promotions took place. Joseph had already had two "promotions" by this time—but only spiritual eyes could discern that.

How God Tests You

God will often test you by first prospering someone else. This principle may even qualify as a spiritual law. If we are going to be Josephs who displace the darkness from the mountains of society, we will have to pass this significant test of selflessness. Can we still be motivated to get up early, to be on time, to keep our word, to work hard when we are doing it for someone else? Can we get joy from seeing those who we are serving prosper because of us while not yet having figured out what's in it for us? This can only happen when our greatest joy is daily fellowship with God and watching Him be famous through the ways He uses us.

This test gets a lot harder when it's complicated by the fact that the person we are blessing is not a Christian. Many of us are glad to serve an Elijah if we can become an Elisha. We willingly serve a Moses in order to be the Joshua. We will submit to a Paul because we are his Timothy. But what about serving a person with no appreciable mantle to leave us? Here is your answer: Joseph served Potiphar, who did nothing for him long term except wrongfully throw him into prison. Joseph had his own intimacy-generated mantle—his coat of many colors—and he could freely serve anyone without hindering his journey toward his destiny.

You may be serving a Potiphar, but if you can determine that the hand of the Lord put you there, you can learn from the life of Joseph. God is about to release situations that will promote you, but beware: these promotions might only seem so in hindsight. In the biblical Joseph's story, the most significant promotion is yet to come. But at first it will not look like a promotion at all.

8

The Potiphar's Wife Test

S CRIPTURE TELLS US that Joseph "was handsome in form and appearance" (Gen. 39:6). Joseph was no longer in the tail of society. He had gone from the flocks to the marketplace and was successfully climbing the mountain of his dreams. The favor of God was so clearly on him that he carried the attraction of the Lord in him. Whenever we find ourselves in this situation, we need to be very aware of the truths of this chapter. We will inevitably face the Potiphar's Wife Test.

> And it came to pass after these things that his master's wife cast longing eyes on Joseph, and she said, "Lie with me." But he refused and said to his master's wife, "Look, my master does not know what is with me in the house, and he has committed all that he has to my hand. There is no one greater in this house than I, nor has he kept back anything from me but you, because you are his wife. How then can I do this great wickedness, and sin against God?" So it was, as she spoke to Joseph day by day, that he did not heed her, to lie with her or to be with her.
>
> —GENESIS 39:7–10

The Lord really is going to fill the mountains of society with Josephs, and we will be His tsunami of blessings to the nations. But as that happens, we'd better understand the spiritual territory we're entering. We'd better have the armor of the spirit that directly corresponds to the spirit operating on the mountain. The higher up the mountains we go, the closer we come to the principality that is ruling illegally there and is dominating the thoughts of men and women in that sphere.

SEDUCTION BY GREED AND/OR LUST

The Potiphar's Wife Test comes when, because of our favor and success, we are catapulted to a place of temptation and seduction. And often we will have to overcome not just an occasional seduction but a constant atmosphere of it. Potiphar's wife spoke to Joseph "day by day" to lie with her. It wasn't a one-time test that he could pass, then say, "Whew, I'm glad that's behind me." Potiphar's wife, literally for him and figuratively for us, is there *every day*. That's why only intimate friends of the Lord will fulfill their Joseph callings.

For example, if you are climbing the mountain of government in God's favor, you will have multiple opportunities to make under-the-table deals that could secure your place in Potiphar's house. Joseph was in a privileged position: "There is no one greater in this house than I," he told Potiphar's wife (Gen. 39:9). Because of his enviable position, it might have even seemed to him that he was fulfilling his original dreams of ruling and having dominion. Potiphar was a very important man. He was an officer of Pharaoh himself and captain of his guard. It could have been easy for Joseph to think that this was as high as he was going to go. It would have been natural for him to think he could secure his place in the house forever by being involved with Potiphar's wife. As long as he wasn't caught—and because he had a lot of latitude in his position over the household, he wouldn't be—he could have secured his destiny. But, of course, that would have been advancing a different kingdom, the one that presently operated on the mountain.

We really must see that we aren't just advancing a "Christian cause." We don't simply need technical, official Christians on the influential mountains of society. Good, faithful Christians already operate in every sphere of society. The problem is that we can be in all the right places but not advancing the right kingdom. That's the real question—which kingdom are we advancing? When we operate as the world does, then we are advancing the world. When we operate according to the demonic powers on a mountain, we are advancing that kingdom of darkness. When we operate in the armor of the spirit that opposes those demonic powers, only then are we expanding the kingdom of God. The kingdom of God advances not in technical identity but in righteous behavior. It is better to have a "non-Christian" president with righteous behavior than a "Christian" president with unrighteous behavior. There is no cause other than the kingdom of God. The first DNA mark of the kingdom of God is righteousness.

> For the kingdom of God is…righteousness and peace and joy in the Holy Spirit.
>
> —ROMANS 14:17

This is very important for us to understand. Though heaven may get populated by decisions for Christ, righteous behavior is what actually advances the kingdom of God on earth. Righteous behavior cannot atone for your sins and give you eternal access into heaven. Only faith in Jesus and His righteous blood can secure eternity for you. But once that is established, only righteous behavior will expand the kingdom. True, sustainable righteousness can only proceed from us as we mature to absolute reliance on the Lord—and that, of course, becomes our ultimate goal. However, as we practically think of the kingdom advancing into society, we must know that the goal is not just placing people who are technically Christians in the right places. The goal is to expound and expand a kingdom way of doing things.

Joseph would have instantly lost all his kingdom authority if he had succumbed to Potiphar's wife. To yield to the spirit operating on the mountain is to begin advancing the enemy's kingdom. Someone who is called to government cannot yield to corruption in any fashion, even though it will be a daily temptation. Someone called to arts and entertainment cannot yield to Jezebel's seductive lusts, though seduction will be there day to day. Those called to access God's economy in business cannot yield to greed, even though greed will be like Potiphar's wife crying out daily, "Please lie with me." People called to the mountain of media cannot yield to the forked tongue that infiltrates virtually all media. One called to work on the mountain of family cannot also be yielding to secret sexual perversions. One called to the mountain of education cannot get in bed with humanism. Nor, finally, can someone called to influence the mountain of religion be seduced by the Potiphar's wife of religious appearance.

Every mountain has its Potiphar's wife, and the higher you go, the more loudly she cries out and the stronger her seductions become. You can prepare your armor by knowing the Potiphar's wife on your mountain and staying clear of her.

We currently have Christians on every mountain who are advancing the other kingdom because they have already fallen to Potiphar's wife, and many don't even know it. Once your righteousness ceases to exceed the environment ruling around you, you are just another vehicle of the dark kingdom. You may be going to heaven when you die, but for now you are advancing the kingdom of Satan. That's harsh, but it's a truth we absolutely have to understand.

In 1900, Christians amounted to one out of every twenty-eight people on the earth. Today we have grown to more than one in every four. Mathematically, we seem to be taking over the world. Yet in terms of righteousness, virtually every mountain of society is in significantly worse shape than it was in 1900. There is more corruption in governments. There is more twisting of the truth in media. There is far more of Jezebel's influence in the arts. Families are substantially more broken and fractured. Greed is much more dominant in our economies. Our educational system is severely more humanistic. But religiosity abounds, and we keep getting "decisions for Christ." We've grown from one in twenty-eight to one in four, yet we can't say that the kingdom of God is more evident. Christianity is growing, but kingdom influence isn't.

Part of the reason for this is that we have recognized only the mountain of religion as a mission field, and part of the reason is that the few of us who have made it to the other mountains have not grasped the mission nor worn the armor required to survive and thrive there. Joseph made it because God was with him. He was a pursuer of God and thus a successful man. We will make it if we have the same priorities.

"AND NONE OF THE MEN OF THE HOUSE WAS INSIDE"

But it happened about this time, when Joseph went into the house
to do his work, and none of the men of the house was inside, that

she caught him by his garment, saying, "Lie with me." But he left
his garment in her hand, and fled and ran outside.

—GENESIS 39:11–12

Potiphar's wife was angered by Joseph's rejection of her advances, and she
falsely accused him before her husband and got him thrown in jail. But
Joseph did make a serious omission that cost him dearly. Though he was
wholly righteous, and though he daily said no to Potiphar's wife, he didn't
take the necessary precautions to keep himself safe. On the surface, it may
not seem that relevant that "none of the men of the house were inside."
But if we consider that Joseph was overseer of everything that happened
in the household, this statement says a lot. Joseph knew where everyone
was working. He also knew that every day that he stepped into that house
Potiphar's wife was going to go after him. With that foreknowledge, his first
precautionary move every day should have been to make sure he wasn't in
there alone with her. He had total power in the household, and someone
within that household was attempting to make him fall from his place
of favor. The higher you go in favor and authority, the more precautions
become necessary.

Joseph should have always been accompanied by another person for two
good reasons. One was to make sure that *his* flesh was never weak enough
that he would compromise; and the second was to make sure he always
had a witness of the actual truth. It is very plausible that the other house
workers knew that Potiphar's wife was interested in Joseph. They might all
have suspected that Joseph was being falsely accused of attempted rape. Yet
Joseph had no witnesses because though he was overseer of everything, he
did not foresee a situation that he should have foreseen. It may seem harsh
to blame Joseph for his lack of foresight, but it was a situation he was daily
facing and not something that just caught him off guard. We must learn
from this story and properly apply it to our lives.

Evangelist Billy Graham had a policy of always having men around him
and never being caught alone. This was something he put into play after he
became well known, of course; it wasn't needed when he was in "the tail."
It was a measure commensurate with the new level of authority and favor
on his life. He placed trusted men around him for two reasons: so his own
flesh would never have to wrestle with whether to yield to a temptation and
so that he could never be falsely accused.

As we go into the head of society, we need to adopt precautionary measures that cover both concerns. Can we be seduced? Can we be falsely accused? When resources no longer become an issue (which happens when you proceed high enough up the mountain), then that becomes the time to implement the new measures commensurate with the favor and authority of the position.

Amazingly, in one day Joseph went from ruler of the house to prison. The very man that had trusted him with oversight of everything was now putting him into jail. He either actually believed his wife or felt that he had to support his wife, as implausible as the accusation sounded. "This 'man of God' could not have done such a thing," Potiphar must have thought. But maybe as he thought through it, it struck him as curious that Joseph would have no one else in the house with him. He knew Joseph was supremely wise and gifted. He knew that God was with Joseph (Gen. 39:3). He knew his house was blessed in all ways because of this man. But maybe he wondered if Joseph had a problem in this one area of temptation.

In the absence of any other witnesses, Joseph went off to prison, apparently now off the fast track to the top of the mountain. Had his destiny been aborted for his oversight? Had his destiny been delayed for his lack of foresight? Before we consider those questions, let's linger on this lesson from this chapter in Joseph's life: the higher you go, the more precautions you must make. That comes with the territory. Potiphar's wife will always be there.

9

The Disguised Promotion of Pharaoh's Prison

Then Joseph's master took him and put him into the prison, a place where the king's prisoners were confined. And he was there in the prison. But the Lord was with Joseph and showed him mercy, and He gave him favor in the sight of the keeper of the prison. And the keeper of the prison committed to Joseph's hand all the prisoners who were in the prison; whatever they did there, it was his doing. The keeper of the prison did not look into anything that was under Joseph's authority, because the Lord was with him; and whatever he did, the Lord made it prosper.

—GENESIS 39:20–23

THESE FOUR VERSES contain a lot of information. Twice they emphasize that the Lord was with Joseph. This continues to be the key to Joseph's life, the reason he wasn't displaced from destiny even when it looked like he would be. The foundation of a living, daily, interactive walk with the Lord sustained and continued to propel him. The fact that the Lord "showed him mercy" is worded appropriately because, in a sense, Joseph deserved this setback by not taking precautionary measures to guard himself from Potiphar's wife. To whom much is given, much is required. But in God's mercy, Joseph got another chance.

"A PLACE WHERE THE KING'S PRISONERS WERE CONFINED"

Joseph would one day realize that Potiphar was the catalyst for his entering the fullness of his destiny. He was now closer than ever to the prophetic dream he had as a youth. Potiphar did not have him thrown into the normal prison. As angry as he might have been with Joseph, something told him that this guy did not belong among that category of prisoners. Joseph would not have normally been grouped with the king's prisoners, but Potiphar, the captain of the guard, made an exception. That meant that this apparent demotion or detour actually put Joseph closer to the mountaintop than he had ever been. To be in Pharaoh's prison was to be potentially just one call from Pharaoh. It's true that this was a heavily disguised promotion, but it was still a promotion. It would turn out to be the last stage before the manifestation of Joseph's full destiny.

The prophetic word of the Lord over Joseph's life was now propelling him into the last stage of process so that he could handle the awesome weight of his destiny. Joseph was going to save the world, and so God had to prepare and refine a world saver. The greater the call, the greater the process. Any destiny that comes easy isn't a very significant destiny.

A painful process means one of two things: either you are being prepared for something very significant or you are reaping what you have sown from the times you have resisted submission to process. This is important to realize. There is a kind of pain and difficulty that arises from submitting to arduous process, and there's also a kind of pain and difficulty in bucking the refining process of the Lord. The difference is that one leads to a significant destiny (and the Lord gets to define *significant*), and the other will end with you still circling in the desert. Submission to process is *the* missing ingredient for many of us.

"THE KING'S PRISONERS WERE CONFINED"

We are taking this phrase on its own merit. King's prisoners are confined. If you have a kingly call and anointing, you will have to submit to intense "confinement" before experiencing the great release of breakthrough. In fact, as we analyze the stages of Joseph's life, we can recognize that the one constant in his refining process was incremental confinement. He started out a free-ranging guy who hung out in the open air among the flocks. Then he was sold to the Midianite traders, who were also prone to moving around, but he was confined to their movements. They then sold him to Potiphar, where he was confined to serving in one house—a nice house in which he had all authority. Then after the incident with Potiphar's wife, he found himself in the greatest confinement of his life. For the first time he was behind bars. He was higher than he had ever been, but he had less freedom than he'd ever had. He would be dealing with people who regularly interacted with the king, and he would get a feel from them of how royal matters took place. If Joseph had sulked at this point in his destiny, this would have been as high as he rose. The rest of his life would have been remembering the "glory days" of Potiphar's house.

Many people—and you may be one of them—are in this last stage. We are in the Joseph years, when God is about to do a wondrous thing. The mountain of His house will be exalted on the tops of the mountains (Isa. 2:2). Those who occupy the mountaintops will have submitted to processes of refinement and confinement. You are not your own. Being in the king's prison precedes being kingly. It is a uniquely designed set of confining circumstances to allow God to do His finishing touches on you. His purpose is to prepare you to survive the weight of your coming destiny. His goal is for you to thrive in what's coming up for you. If you sulk, the "keeper of the prison" will not position you for the last stage of your destiny. If you are somehow able to escape on your own, you will have just lost the vehicle of promotion. If you are able to manipulate yourself around this last test, you'll be unprepared. You will fall once you're "in power" and bring disgrace to yourself and to God. You will have missed the fact that you were in the oven but weren't done yet.

The fast track to destiny is submission to the process. God offers two things through the course of the entire matter. One, He will be with you if you will be with Him. When that becomes our greatest joy, the pain of the process loses its sting. Two, we can still have the favor of the many-colored coat He gave us. Joseph continued to be a successful man because he was grounded in these two things.

"AND HE GAVE HIM FAVOR"

Joseph was confined, but God's favor was still available to him as long as he stayed in process. Joseph did not sulk but decided to live off that which always sustained him—his intimate relationship with the Lord. Part of the silver lining of this test was that he no longer faced the daily temptations of Potiphar's wife. In Potiphar's house, his character was being tested. In refusing her and fleeing the situation, he had won some level of victory. In prison, the primary test was a test of faith. Here was Joseph, the dreamer who dreamed of ruling and reigning, and he had never been less free. Even worse, he was there *because* he was so righteous. He had to be wondering if God was still in charge. Joseph was now about ten years into being almost perfect, and yet prison seemed to be the antithesis of reigning. How could a guy called to dominion have spent ten years being as faithful as possible, only to find himself in terrible circumstances? Hindsight helps us realize that Joseph was actually very close to the top at this point. But going through it, his situation looked like the greatest contradiction imaginable.

A significant key to passing your tests is recognizing the Lord and His favor in the midst of them. Of course, this favor is only for His Josephs. Only Joseph got the coat of many colors. Only Joseph got the seven mountain mantle. "Leah's sons" still get to go to heaven, but they don't get the mantle. They don't even have a vision for why a mantle is necessary. They aren't trying to displace anything; they just want to survive until evacuation day. They have one vision and one hope: don't get left behind. Not much process is required for this vision because the vision is as weak as Leah's eyes. It's a very popular vision, though; it sells lots of books and movie tickets. When all you live for is checking out, you'll hang out at the bottom of the mountain, roaming with the flock, occasionally finding someone else to get in the checkout line with you. In a ten-to-one ratio, Jacob's sons choose this mentality. That's why when Jacob found a son who thought differently, he put a distinguishing mantle on him.

"EVERYTHING WAS UNDER JOSEPH'S AUTHORITY"

Depending on how Joseph looked at his life, he was either in prison or practicing governing. All was placed under Joseph, and the keeper of the prison "did not look into anything…because the LORD was with him" (Gen. 39:23). This was a virtual repeat scenario of what took place in Potiphar's house. Joseph's administrative gift was so anointed and founded in supernatural wisdom that the keeper of the prison just turned *everything* over to him.

As it applies to us today, the Joseph anointing at its core is not specifically an anointing to make money. Rather, it's an administrative gift that is so supernatural that people trust you enough to turn everything over to you. Joseph had received no training in prison management, just as he never received training in how to run Potiphar's house. Reading leadership books will give you a lot of great tips and strategies, but only supernatural favor that comes from an intimacy mantle can cause you to be a real difference-maker.

All true authority comes from God. His principles only get you onto the playing field. You won't do well in running His plays unless you stay in constant contact with Him and expect Him to keep communicating with you. You can no more play sports by principles than can you live by principles. Principles are a starting point—in fact, that's the literal meaning of the word—but you play an entire game based on the present score and how much time is left, who was injured, who still feels strong, who is having a good or bad day. Things like the rhythm of a game or momentum swings can never be addressed by principles established before the game. A Joseph knows the principles but lives in the fluidity of life, which dictates that he must have constant contact, feedback, interaction, and encouragement from Coach. That's where a supernatural gift of administration comes from. You can't just study to be a good administrator; you must live in the gift.

The gift of administration is actually a gift of stewardship. Joseph first gave evidence of this when at seventeen he gave his father a bad report on his brothers' flock-keeping prowess. He wasn't a tattletale; he was just wired differently. He saw a bunch of brothers just going through the motions. He was appalled at their lack of vision. His stewardship DNA came out of who he was and not something he specifically was taught. Being a product of the "Rachel church," he had a different lens for viewing life and why we are here.

Josephs are motivated by a passion for *God* to be made famous in all the earth. Victorious eschatology flows through the blood in a Joseph's veins. The whole earth will one day be filled with the glory of God, and God places

His sons and daughters here to be the carriers of this glory. I believe Isaiah 2:2 was already oozing from Joseph's veins back in Genesis. He seemed to know that one day God's house and His people would be exalted at the tops of the dominant sectors of society, and all nations would come running. Joseph was a man ahead of his time, and he brought ahead-of-his-time changes upon society.

"Whatever He Did, the Lord Made It Prosper"

The Lord has made an enviable place available for us—a place where we are so wired to Him and so in tune with who He is and what He is doing that He causes everything we do to prosper. This is a relational privilege that He has ahead for us.

Many of us are afflicted by the questions, Am I doing what God wants me to do? Is God going to bless this venture I'm heading into? We may consider these to be the primary questions we are facing. If we knew that He was going to back us, then we would be OK. Can you imagine entering the privileged place where everything we do, He makes it prosper? Joseph entered into this dimension while he was still in fetters and irons.

> They hurt his feet with fetters, He was laid in irons. Until the time that his word came to pass, The word of the Lord tested him. The king sent and released him.
>
> —Psalm 105:18–20

A Joseph people birthed from a Rachel church will grow into a place of such relational harmony with God and His vision for the nations that the desires of their heart begin to be His desires. He longs for a people who so clearly see what He is doing that He may back their initiatives, which come out of His DNA within them. He is not looking for robots who just know how to obey commands. The obedience that He looks for is obedience to DNA—who He is when He manifests through us. He wants obedience to His creative genius *in us*—Christ in us, the hope of glory. He's not looking for our creative genius that comes independently of Him. That was Abraham's idea when he went to Hagar and attempted to birth the promise. It is as we partner with Him, as we are one with Him, as we relate intimately to Him, that Christ is formed in us. Then He can trust the dreams and passions that we get "pregnant" with, and even though they are growing in us and will manifest through us, He will prosper them. This is a place of relational privilege. It is the favor of the coat of many colors.

10

The Fulfillment of Dreams

And Pharaoh said to his servants, "Can we find such a one as this, a man in whom is the Spirit of God?" Then Pharaoh said to Joseph, "Inasmuch as God has shown you all this, there is no one as discerning and wise as you. You shall be over my house, and all my people shall be ruled according to your word; only in regard to the throne will I be greater than you." And Pharaoh said to Joseph, "See, I have set you over all the land of Egypt."

—GENESIS 41:38–41

THIS PASSAGE DESCRIBES the precise moment when Joseph was promoted to the position of power that he had prophetically dreamed of as a teenager, but it didn't come easily or immediately. First, he had to endure a little more process while he was still in prison. Pharaoh's chief butler and chief baker had fallen out of favor, and they were cast into prison with Joseph. While in prison, they each had a dream that could only be interpreted by the prophetic guy incarcerated with them. Joseph informed them of the good news/bad news scenarios facing them. They would both be called back before Pharaoh within three days; the butler would be restored to his position, but the baker would be hanged. It happened just as Joseph said, and now Joseph had more reason to hope. He had told the butler to mention him to Pharaoh. It appeared that his confinement and refinement would finally be over. But it wasn't quite time yet. The chief butler forgot about him.

Joseph was by then twenty-eight, and things seemed to be going nowhere. It had been eleven years since his vivid prophetic dreams of ruling and reigning. How long would he be forgotten? Two more years went by—or, as the Scripture says, two *full* years. His father, Jacob, had served seven years for Rachel; that time had only seemed like a few days, but these two years did not fly by. They dragged on and on and tested the very foundation of who Joseph was. He had his own moments of wondering, "My God, my God, why have You forsaken Me?"—the cry of anguish Jesus uttered from the cross (Matt. 27:46). The greatest destiny will almost always be preceded by a cross experience in which God seems to have forgotten His servant.

"THEY BROUGHT HIM QUICKLY OUT OF THE DUNGEON"

> Then Pharaoh sent and called Joseph, and they brought him quickly out of the dungeon; and he shaved, changed his clothing, and came to Pharaoh. And Pharaoh said to Joseph, "I have had a dream, and there is no one who can interpret it. But I have heard it said of you that you can understand a dream, to interpret it."
>
> —GENESIS 41:14–15

Upon hearing that Pharaoh had had some troubling dreams, the butler suddenly remembered Joseph and informed Pharaoh about him. Joseph was quickly brought before the king. His time came only when society was facing crisis. Two years earlier, Pharaoh wasn't ready to hear from a Joseph. Now he was. It was God's divine timetable.

By then, it had been fourteen years since Joseph's teenage dreams. His father, Jacob, had had to work fourteen years for his Rachel. Joseph was now going to be leading and governing society in the most critical fourteen-year period of the age. These numbers are significant. The four sevens that showed up on the stock market on September 29, 2008—the 777.7-point drop in the Dow Jones average—confirmed to me that we have entered the Joseph years. I believe that the first two sevens of the Josephs have already taken place and that we have now entered the second set of sevens. The last sign Joseph saw that let him know his destiny was near was the hanging of the chief baker. The chief "bread maker" had failed. Bread would have to be made in a new way. I'll take parabolic liberty to say we are presently in a society facing a failure of the "bread making." The economy is broken, and Joseph solutions are sorely in need. As I write this, we have been in two years of a broken economy since a recession started in 2007, and Joseph's time has come.

I believe we will see a prophetic fulfillment of the above Scripture verses in the coming days. Society will quickly call for Josephs to come deal with unprecedented and impossible situations. Many dungeon denizens will be suddenly called for such a time as this. Believe it and trust God to supply your "new clothes" at the right moment.

"Joseph Was Thirty Years Old When He Stood Before Pharaoh"

> Joseph was thirty years old when he stood before Pharaoh king
> of Egypt. And Joseph went out from the presence of Pharaoh,
> and went throughout all the land of Egypt.
>
> —Genesis 41:46

It had to seem initially to Joseph as if difficult people in his life had delayed his destiny. First, his brothers hated him and put him in a pit. Then they sold him to some Midianites and lied to his father that he had been killed. The Midianites then sold him to Potiphar. Potiphar's wife then falsely accused him of rape, and he got thrown in the dungeon. Just when he thought he might be catching up on his perceived timetable, the butler forgot him for two years. Treason, treachery, betrayal, envy, false accusation by everyone around him—yet he was perfectly on time. Only God could impose this kind of sovereignty in a free-will world.

Can you believe in a God big enough to superimpose His timing of destiny on your life when you are surrounded by a bunch of losers? Do you feel that your pastor or your boss has held you back? Do you think sexism or racism has hindered your destiny? Do you feel that circumstances have waylaid you? Remember Joseph. If God is with you because you are with Him, and if you can be a successful person—someone who has a profound relationship with God and who hears His voice and obeys Him—you'll find the timing of breakthrough in your life being divinely orchestrated. God can even help you make up time for your own failures. He's big enough even for that. Even Joseph had a careless moment with Potiphar's wife, yet the Lord had mercy on him and didn't allow him to be late. The main key is to be a Joseph, and that invitation is for everyone. God doesn't have favorites in the sense of only inviting select people to be Josephs. He invites everyone. But those who respond to Him become His favorites. We need to get out of Leah's house and get into Rachel's house. He loves Leah and will have children with her, but He is smitten with Rachel. His heart pounds in response to her. He's a relationally minded and motivated God.

"PHARAOH CALLED JOSEPH'S NAME ZAPHNATH-PAANEAH"

We are told of Joseph's not-so-catchy name in Genesis 41:45, and it doesn't seem very relevant. But there's great significance in this name. Pharaoh's naming of Joseph made a pretty powerful statement. The Egyptian name has many meanings, among them "God speaks and lives" or "savior of the age." Joseph was evidence to Pharaoh and society that there is a God, and that not only does He speak and live, He also has a heart to save society.

We must understand the implications of this as a parable for us today. The nations will run to the mountain of the house of the Lord because of the saving wisdom and administration coming from it. We are to model and reveal a God who speaks into the affairs of human beings and brings His wisdom to thrive here on earth. There is a wisdom from God that can cause governments to function correctly here on earth. There is a creativity from Him that can outshine all other forms of distorted creativity modeled in the world. God has an economic structure and plan that can work here on earth. We even have the foundation of it written on the backs of our dollar bills—"in God we trust." All mountains of society will one day show-case the God of glorious solutions.

Isaiah 60:3 tells us that "kings will come to the brightness of our rising" (author's paraphrase). Government leaders will urgently call for Josephs, and Josephs will come with a primary focus of saving the age and not just preparing for the hereafter. Jesus knew that this could and would happen and therefore declared, "Your kingdom come...On earth as it is in heaven" (Matt. 6:9; Luke 11:2). Let the functions and purposes of heaven's rule descend to earth. Let the ways of heaven's government come to earth. Let the way creativity is showcased in heaven come to earth. Let the relational glory of family come to earth. Let the economic structure of heaven's provision come down to earth.

When we receive nations as inheritance, we have to run them with a bigger agenda than "sign on the dotted line so you won't go to hell when you die." Heaven has an order or discipline that will work here on earth. The Great Commission to go and disciple nations means, "Bring the discipline of heaven to earth." Satan will oppose it, but the nations will run to it. Jesus is the desire of *all* nations (Hag. 2:7). The way His kingdom operates in heaven will also work here.

> Then Pharaoh took his signet ring off his hand and put it on Joseph's hand; and he clothed him in garments of fine linen and put a gold chain around his neck. And he had him ride in the second chariot which he had; and they cried out before him, "Bow the knee!" So he set him over all the land of Egypt.
>
> —GENESIS 41:42–43

Joseph was now in the season of the fulfillment of his dreams. All were commanded to bow before him. His brothers would be coming soon and doing the same, thus fulfilling what they would never have imagined. Joseph had gone through such an intense process that he no longer cared about someone bowing before him. He had been on the other end of this spectrum for the last thirteen years. He had been in chains, and he had been doing the bowing. He was just glad to be a free man. He was glad that God was using his prophetic gift to decipher heaven's solution for rescuing the nations. Egypt would be saved by Joseph's plan, but the nations would come to him as the famine spread. All economic systems that did not flow from God's wisdom would collapse. But a Joseph who knew how to handle the dreams of God would bring the solutions, not just for his family and people but for the nations.

Over the seven-year period that began with Rosh Hashanah 2008 and will continue to Rosh Hashanah 2015—though its characteristics and influence will extend well beyond that—we will see an army of Josephs begin to be raised up into the seven mountains of society. In Part II of this book, we will explore what that will look like. We will address each of the seven mountains and reveal prophetic breakthroughs that will come on them.

This is a most exciting time for the Rachel church and the Joseph people who will come out of her. The invitation goes out to all of God's children, but only the Josephs will receive His coat of many colors. Only those who choose to be His Josephs will begin to dream His dreams for the nations. It will be absolutely awesome.

Part II

What It Looks Like Today

11

Seven Years of Plenty

WAS AWAKENED AT 3:43 a.m. in December 2008, and the Lord instructed me to go look at Psalm 34:3: "Oh, magnify the LORD with me, And let us exalt His name together." The Lord began to speak to me:

> My people are magnifying their fears, their doubts, their concerns, their anxieties. I am very large for them at this time, and I need you to tell them to magnify Me so that they will see Me the size that I actually am. For those who get a vision of my true size, I will cause these next seven years to be seven years of plenty. I have one quadrillion dollars of resources that I am making available for my Josephs. A treasure chest has been made available as of Rosh Hashanah 2008 [September 29, the day Wall Street Dow Jones fell a record 777.7 points], and it will be open until Rosh Hashanah 2015. I am longing to show Myself strong and large to My people and to the nations as a God of provision during these seven years. Many of my people have known that there will be an End time transfer of wealth, but they have been fishing in the wrong pond. Wall Street is not the source from which my one quadrillion dollars of resources will come. I have many other ways of providing wealth. My Joseph dreams will be coming to my sons and daughters, and I will have strategies, inventions, and hidden treasures of every kind available to be discovered.

I received more on this as I further communed with the Lord. I was blown away with the "quadrillion" number. I can't remember having even thought of that number since childhood, when I was intrigued by big numbers. A quadrillion is a 1 followed by 15 zeros. It's a thousand trillion, and I believe it greatly exceeds the known household wealth of the entire world. I don't know if the Lord was giving me a literal number or just telling me He has inexhaustible resources. Either way, it's more than we can comprehend.

Let me be clear that this is not about Christians becoming wealthy for the sake of wealth. Some believers seek prosperity for themselves—to be reservoirs of wealth rather than conduits of it. God's resources are being made available to Josephs who see their role as those who bless society and advance the kingdom through their generosity. God makes His treasures available to those who will know what to do with them to accomplish His purposes.

I have some understanding and history in seeing extraordinary, supernatural wealth. I have accurately prophesied the discovery in other nations of three specific gold mines, a silver mine, a zinc mine, two salt mines, and other treasures that are valued in excess of 500 billion dollars. Besides that, I prophesied the discovery of a lost city of an Incan or pre-Incan civilization, which was discovered within eighteen months of the prophecy. It's a city of twenty-five square miles that, when fully accessed and opened up, could potentially become as popular as Machu Picchu, the number one touristic attraction in South America. I have not seen it yet, though I was less than twenty miles from the spot where I prophesied about it, but those who have seen it say there are aspects of it that are more impressive than Machu Picchu. This ancient city has an incalculable value. I say these things simply to establish that it is not hard for me to believe that the Lord can reveal treasures. In addition, I have several friends and acquaintances from different nations that have testified of how God lead them to amazing treasures.

One friend in another country was instructed by the Lord to buy a certain mountain. Then he was given specific instructions of how many steps to walk off in different directions. He then put an X in one spot and called it "Jehovah One," and then was given another spot and called it "Jehovah Two." He then dug in both places and discovered great quantities of gold. He is very wealthy now, and it has been prophesied that he will be the wealthiest man in his nation. He has the "golden goose" of receiving and understanding the dreams of the Lord.

In a different country, another two young ladies who are sisters have a similar testimony. They were so poor as teenagers that they lived in a car for a few years and cried daily, wondering why God had made them. The Lord told them never to cry about that again because He was going to do amazing things with their lives. They now own several gold mines, have hundreds of employees, and own a nine-story building in the most expensive area of their country. They were led to all of their treasures through dreams and other confirming visions from God. God loves doing this kind of stuff. He just wants to get His children to come to Him. Provision is not just something He does, it's who He is. These are just a couple of many examples; God is doing this with many other people.

Let me be clear that the Joseph anointing is not specifically an anointing to make wealth. It is rather a calling to meet a need in such a unique way that wealth is simply a byproduct. We see in Joseph's story that he was never just trying to figure out how to increase wealth. He provided a solution to a potential crisis, and wealth was the byproduct. It is imperative for rising Josephs to see that they are called not to seek riches but to meet needs in uncommon, unique, brilliant, God-inspired ways. When they do, a financial bonanza will frequently accompany the solution and become an additional blessing.

2008-2011: GETTING THE NEW WINESKIN

I believe that during the first three years of this seven-year period, only about 10 percent of rising Josephs will see radical breakthroughs. Most of you will be going through a period of rewiring by the Lord during which He will produce the new wineskin in you so you can handle the new wine that is coming. For that reason, many of you will feel much the way Joseph felt before he was brought before Pharaoh. But if you understand and embrace the process, you will see that He is doing a quick work. The ahead-of-schedule Josephs will be very important in opening up paths and doors for a potential multitude to follow.

Much of the rewiring will come as Josephs allow themselves to receive and digest the seven mountain message that preceded this book. I recommend reading my book *The Seven Mountain Prophecy* and also the material my friend Lance Wallnau has produced related to this subject. Receiving a new paradigm for life and ministry does not come easily, but these will help you change the way you think. I have read my own book five times in

English and two times in Spanish, despite having received the revelation myself and having preached it in many nations. Why? Because I want to be more thoroughly saturated in it. It takes time to unlearn one wineskin and learn a new one. The old eschatology that put so much focus on the Antichrist has to be eradicated, and we need to adopt a new eschatology that focuses on a glorious breaking into a new age.

I want to close this chapter with a verse that the Lord has been repeatedly giving me recently. For our purposes, it stands alone as a "now" word for us.

> Look among the nations and watch—Be utterly astounded! For
> I will work a work in your days which you would not believe,
> though it were told you.
> —HABAKKUK 1:5

The work that the Lord is going to do will be so astounding that almost none of us could possibly have imagined it. We wouldn't believe it even if it were told to us. He is going to do a work among the nations that is exceedingly, abundantly above what we have been able to even dream. We will begin getting His astounding dreams, and we will begin climbing the mountains of society with unprecedented favor and glory. He will place on us a mantle for a most amazing work. The life of Joseph is the closest example that could give us a grid to understand how astounding it will be.

Over the next seven chapters, I will take a closer look at each mountain of society and describe some of the advances and breakthroughs that I see Josephs having on them. This will be a starting point for understanding some of the trends of God in each sector. For some, it will confirm some things God is already speaking to you. For others, it will be godly fertilizer for a dream life that will begin to consume you. He wants to partner with all of us in amazing ways.

12

Joseph on the Mountain of Government

I N MY BOOK *The Seven Mountain Prophecy*, I describe the usurping principality on the mountain of government, Lucifer, and the lies and tactics that he uses: pride and corruption. I also explain the apostolic mantle available to displace the darkness from this mountain. Lucifer will be removed by those who ascend the mountain of government in a spirit opposite to his pride, a spirit of humility and service. True apostles, those who function in that role as Scripture defines it, will be instrumental in this area of society. They will understand that "of the increase of [Jesus'] government there will be no end" (Isa. 9:7).

Here I want to specifically describe the Joseph movements that will be taking place on this mountain over our current seven-year period (2008–2015), even though we are already well into that period.

RETHINKING HOW TO GAIN POLITICAL ACCESS

In the old wineskin of thought, a conventional approach for gaining access to political power was getting an Ivy League education in political science, law, or economics, followed by political internships and then a steady climb up the mountain. The rules of access have already changed. You now have a better chance at becoming president by having celebrity status than you do for your qualifications. President Barack Obama had the least amount of governmental experience of any candidate of either party when he ran. But he carried a celebrity factor that our pop culture can rapidly cultivate, and that trumped over all other factors. Sarah Palin was a major threat to Democratic candidates and issues because of the same celebrity factor. Her policies and skills weren't that different from other conservatives; it was her popular appeal that scared the left. Arnold Schwarzenegger is governor of California for similar reasons. This celebrity status can be a result of God's favor, or it can come from slick packaging and marketing appeal to the masses.

Because of less traditional paths leading to political influence, you can be the most qualified politician on the planet and not get very far if you aren't likeable. Conversely, a well-crafted, ten-minute YouTube speech by a person with a likeability factor could propel that person into the national political spotlight virtually overnight. We can either gripe and complain about that or just realize that it is what it is—and that it actually opens up unprecedented possibilities for Josephs to come from out of nowhere into prominence.

RETHINKING TRADITIONAL CONSERVATIVE BATTLEFIELDS

In the old wineskin of thought, our biggest political battlefields would start with the issue of abortion and then marriage between homosexuals. The next battlefield might be stem-cell research. Another common conservative platform is the idea of smaller government. We've been strong on pushing for prayer in public schools and opposing the teaching of evolution without also teaching creationism. We've assumed that if our conservative candidates don't show up dressed in the merit badges of these arguments, they might as well not show up at all.

I believe we need to rethink battlefields that don't give us a legitimate chance at a national platform. If society undergoes a great awakening toward righteousness, then we may have success on these traditional battlefields. But until that happens, we need to take a new approach, an approach that doesn't attempt to impose morality on people who have no grid for it. That's the fear of those in love with their sins; our moral positions mean nothing to them. But there are innovative political strategies—Joseph-style approaches—that disarm the spiritual enemies who are resisting us on present battlefields and that create new battlefields where the enemy has not yet gathered his troops.

The Abortion Battlefield

First of all, the new Josephs in government need not show up with their opposition to abortion as their number one calling card. We currently have two opposing armies positioned on the battlefield: the pro-life forces and the pro-choice forces. Perhaps a rising Joseph should advocate a "pro-responsible-choice" platform. This would make it legal to get an abortion as long as the patient has viewed a video that shows what her fetus looks like at its current stage of growth and that shows an actual abortion being performed. This measure alone would do more to prevent abortions than any new law. The new battlefield strategy has to focus on the hearts and minds of the people and not seek empty legal victories. Abortions will decrease when this becomes our primary strategy, as opposed to just trying to go after the Supreme Court. It's technically possible to win the Supreme Court battle by getting *Roe v. Wade* reversed and still end up with more abortions being performed illegally. A legal win is important, but it's much less important than a victory in the hearts and minds of people.

A good example of this principle is the issue of illegal drugs. The use of certain drugs is banned by law, but that legal victory doesn't accomplish very much because of the moral vacuum surrounding illicit drug activity. Laws are not the key variable. Fractured families do more to promote abortions and illegal drug use than laws can do to stop them. Therefore, laws that strengthen and protect families will do more to reduce abortions and drug use than laws specifically targeting these issues will. We eventually want to have good laws on the books in all of these areas; that's the desired goal. But simply prohibiting activities without changing hearts is ultimately a futile battle.

The question is not whether abortion is wrong; that's 100 percent clear to anyone who really sees what is taking place. The question is how can we wisely go about reducing this obviously wrong operation. The major goal is for deadened consciences to be pricked and for righteousness to sink into minds and hearts. The new strategy should encompass just how do we do that.

I strongly believe that we have over-mobilized on this battlefield in a way that may result in a shallower victory than we hope for, should we finally "win." Prior to *Roe v. Wade*, we were a pro-life nation, but those who lived then know that we were hardly a picture of the kingdom of God on earth.

The fact that the abortion rate among Christians today is about as high as the rate among non-Christians should tell us we are losing that battle in our own backyard. We have a morality crisis in the church, not just outside of it, and this is our central problem. We have a Christianity that is defined by one-time decisions for Christ rather than by establishing kingdom attitudes within us and a practical kingdom culture among us.

Though our faith is the key to populating heaven, we haven't been very good at manifesting a practical culture of proper behavior on earth. The Protestant Reformation turned our attention against salvation by works so intensely and thoroughly that we have lost the "salt" of our ways. Only faith in Jesus' finished work on the cross can get us into heaven, but we can only displace the effects of evil in our culture by manifesting His righteous ways. To put it more simply, faith gets you into heaven, while works bring heaven to earth. The light of proper Christian works, as seen in our character and integrity, has become so dim that we are losing our culture. Evil laws aren't the main problem; the laws are simply reflecting the glaring reality of how we have fallen short in our works. We have easily enough Christians in the United States to change laws—if we were to agree on a common cause. But we aren't agreeing on common causes because we practice a watered-down, prostituted version of Christianity.

The good news is that this will all change because God is waking us up to His seven mountain purposes on earth. We are to receive and activate the kingdom on earth as it is in heaven. This is what wins the hearts and minds of people, beginning with our own.

The Homosexual Battlefield

Unfortunately, our defense of traditional marriage has been distorted into an anti-homosexual agenda, at least in the hearts and minds of homosexuals who are in need of Christ's acceptance and love. We must regroup and reposition ourselves in this important arena.

A very intentional and scarily efficient homosexual agenda has been playing out for some time now. An activist group representing less than 4 percent (and maybe as low as 2 percent) of the population has targeted the mountains of influence and brought great advances for their cause. One would think that homosexuals make up virtually half of the population based on their cultural impact, but they are statistically very minor. Their ability to pool resources, energy, and focus has allowed them to have an uncanny persuasive effect on culture.

As Christians, we have begun to engage with them on the battlefield by trying to pool our resources, energy, and focus to win legal victories. Again, I see a need for us to beware of hollow victories in which we win a legal battle but lose the hearts and minds not just of homosexuals but of others observing the battle. I'm aware that we are being forced to win some of these legal battles just to keep homosexual indoctrination from being imposed upon our children. It is my belief that a very high percentage of homosexuals suffer from profound feelings of rejection. Broken families, molestation, and the absence (or perceived absence) of a true father are primary causes of homosexuality. I freely admit that I can't back this up by direct statistics, because even the statistics have been politicized and distorted. But I firmly believe this based on my personal interaction with those who have struggled with homosexuality and on various studies I've seen. A statistical survey won't confirm this unless it could command a greater honesty from homosexuals than they might be willing to give. Regardless, my point is that those who are able to receive the unconditional love of the Father can experience dramatic healing from this lifestyle. I've seen that happen again and again.

This is one of those issues that must be fought on several mountains. There are legal battlefields on the mountain of government, but the primary battles on this issue are on the mountain of family and the mountain of religion. As we've recently discovered, some of our brightest and best ministers have struggled with homosexuality. They know and preach about salvation through Jesus Christ, but the personal rejection they may have experienced, combined with the weak nature of our current kingdom culture, has shown that homosexuality is not just a problem "out there" but a significant matter "in here." We have very little moral authority to attempt to impose "out there" what isn't working "in here." I believe that our present Christian culture has actually exacerbated the homosexual problem. Personal family hypocrisy, religion without power and presence, and an emphasis on symbolic "decisions" for Christ over substantive lifestyle adjustments all combine to make a recipe for producing children with the identity crises that lead to homosexuality.

The Lord is going to raise up Josephs who will uniquely meet the needs of this niche of society. Josephs on the mountain of government, Josephs on the mountain of family, and Josephs on the mountain of religion will all receive the dreams of the Father to bring redemptive, restorative strategies and battle plans for recovering that which has been lost in this arena. The "homosexual problem" requires a multipronged battle approach, and we need to be clear that the battle is not against homosexuals themselves. They are in desperate need of the love of the Father. Josephs will receive revelation on how to meet that need while still addressing the problem.

Within ten years, it will be conclusively established that healing for homosexuals is possible and that God has the power to rewire brains in such a way as to reinstall their originally designed sex drive. Along with that, a sweeping move of God will pave the way for those who most need to experience the love of the Father. Love, healing, and solutions will come from God's house to restore the most rejected of society into a place of wholeness with Him and of wholeness with society itself. This will be the most effective response to the homosexual agenda and must be our long-term focus. The homosexual agenda is a radical plan of action designed to garner acceptance, but at its core, this is a spiritual cry, not a political one. Political acceptance still will not satisfy the haunting emptiness of the lifestyle. Let us wage this battle with wisdom—especially from the mountain of government.

The School Prayer Battlefield

It's time for us to be honest enough to acknowledge that the battle for prayer in public schools has largely been a symbolic battle. Real prayer in school simply can't be stopped. As long as there are tests, there will be prayer. But the idea that we have to allow or institute a state- or teacher-led prayer session is folly. The United States is now such a melting pot of religions that we would have to enable all represented religions to have the same right in schools. If we ever happened to win the legal right to have Christian prayers spoken everyday in classrooms, it would be a hollow victory. We will have trampled over the right for people to have freedom of religious choice, which is also a God-given right. We need to get the crusader mentality out of our approach to this issue. It is no more of a righteous attempt than the crusades were. The kingdom of God does not advance through overt imposition. The only kind of imposition that will ever work is when His righteous judgments on the earth convince the lost of their need to follow Him.

Having said that, I do believe there's a Joseph solution to this issue. Christians could team up with Hindus, Muslims, Jews, and anyone else to request freedom for prayer meetings outside of normal school hours. I realize that measures of this are already legally secured, but in various states there are significant restrictions. If Christians request a right that we are ready to defend for other religions, too, no one can be accused of "imposing" anything. Schools should not be legally allowed to squelch such prayer initiatives. That's an issue worth pursuing legally and politically, though not as a major, primary battlefield. The Lord has allowed for the nations and their religions to be drawn to the U.S., and it's important for us to model before them a religion that does not fear competition. This could even be one of the initial attractions of Christianity for those groaning under the bondage of forced religion. The yoke of religion is truly unsatisfying, and Christianity must not be modeled with that kind of yoke.

RETHINKING THE REJECTION OF LIBERAL SOCIAL POLITICS

We Christians can no longer be seen as the lesser voices in matters of social justice and preservation of the planet. Many of the distorted perspectives from liberal camps come in the absence of any substantive voice from Christian or conservative circles. We have spent nearly all of our prayers, fasting, resources, protests, and other energy on the battlefields of abortion and homosexuality. As a result, we have left other significant battlefields unmanned.

I believe our Rapture mentality has directly played into our under-caring for the well-being of the earth and for social injustice in general. Our subconscious mentality is that problems are good because they are signs of Jesus coming soon. Other than seeking decisions for Christ, we have not addressed social ills because our hope in the Rapture is predicated on societal collapse of some nature or another. Many don't want to fix the injustices on the mountain of economy because they have believed a lie that it's all going to end up as a one-world economy anyway. In other words, the sooner we're faced with the economic mark of the beast, the sooner we'll realize our hope of the Rapture. We are consciously or subconsciously expecting the Antichrist, the beast, the false prophet, and the one-world government to ultimately mess up any social repairing we do anyway, so why bother? But that old wineskin of thought must be eradicated by the new rising Josephs on the mountain of government.

In many ways, we would have been dangerous on this mountain if we'd had more recent success. With an eschatology that believes things getting worse means that Jesus must be about to return, we are precluded from pursuing sustained reformation. In terms of approach, some of us are not far removed from Iran's radical president, Mahmoud Ahmadinejad. He wants to push the envelope on world events so that Islam's messiah will come and save the day. He has described a nuclear attack on Jerusalem as a win-win situation. If he is successful in destroying Israel, then he has wrought a great thing for Muslims; and if he's wrong and Israel nukes Iran, then it will force their Mahdi to show up and rescue them.

One reason we haven't had Christian/conservative political leaders with winning ideas is that our ideas show that we don't really believe societal change can be addressed in any other way than in decisions for Christ. That will greatly change during this seven-year period.

THE AWAKENING BETWEEN NOW AND 2015

As this new seven mountain paradigm invades the body of Christ, many rising Josephs will be equipped to make unprecedented political break-throughs. Many nations will form new political parties based on this new paradigm. Most will have a political name that carries the words *reform*, *reformation*, or *restoration* in it. These parties will not be Christian parties per se but rather kingdom-minded parties. They will understand the value in operating in a stealth fashion and in being as "wise as serpents and harmless as doves" (Matt. 10:16). These parties will explode from colleges and universities as a new generation gets a vision and faith to see and be part of what God is doing on earth.

This political movement will not be blatantly Christian, but it will be blatantly moral. In many nations, the movement will gain almost overnight favor to be in power as its leaders carry the Joseph mantle of favor. Even in nations where they don't immediately win elections, they will begin to set the political agenda through their discourse. They will carry an anointing of spiritual reformation that will penetrate every sector of society. They will win just by setting the agenda of dialogue. They will be highly organized, highly motivated, and highly connected to media outlets. They will even create their own media outlets characterized by credibility, and from this platform they will continue in influence and power, even when they don't win elections. They will carry a positive spiritual energy and be noted for their sense of humor and joy in the midst of fierce battles. The way they battle will win over as many hearts and minds as the message they carry. Hope will radiate from them and all will see that God is with them.

This seven mountain political move of God will have five specific approaches or mission fields on the mountain of government.

The candidates division will prepare those who intend to run for office and win elections.

The division of political assistants and advisers will prepare people to remain behind the scenes but help give continuity to the movement. There will be a time in the U.S. when political advisory positions will be filled with Josephs. Even as the biblical Joseph basically ruled from his adviser position, so too will these Josephs.

The division of intercessors will give themselves almost exclusively to praying for this mountain and will link up with candidates and advisers.

The division of financers will be composed of people who recognize the need and their call to provide resources for political Josephs.

A lawmaking division will try to establish righteous laws and eliminate unjust ones independently of elections and other political matters. A unique blend of legal minds will team up with godly celebrities who will help win public support.

It won't be necessary for everyone in these five sectors to be Christian. They simply need to hold certain kingdom values. National reformation does not come by conversions but by exalting righteousness in practical ways. If Mormons will do that better than Christians, let them rule. If Catholics will do that better than evangelicals, then let them rule. There isn't a Christian kingdom, only the kingdom of God. It isn't about Christian causes; it's about getting things to function on earth as they do in heaven. God's kingdom advances in righteousness, peace, and joy. The nations will be attracted to that because He is the desire of *all* nations (Hag. 2:7). A kingdom culture doesn't operate because Christians are in power but because kingdom righteousness and justice are implemented. The *righteous* will inherit the earth. To those who are planning on hanging around a little while, the Lord says, "Ask of Me, and I will give you the nations for your inheritance" (Ps. 2:8).

If you have been trying to squelch your dreams of being involved in politics and government because it isn't "holy" or considered real ministry, stop. God is calling you to this mountain. Now is the time to rope yourself to fellow mountaineers. You don't climb mountains alone—that's treacherous. God will provide the divine companions you need. He will put them together quickly. He is much more interested in godly government than we have been. If you have dreams of influencing this sector of society, He has probably planted them within you. He will help you fulfill them.

13

Joseph on the Mountain of Education

THE DREAMS OF God will soon overtake the rising Josephs who are called to be educators in our society. Our present educational system is in a state of crisis that will continue until Joseph solutions are brought into it. One in three teens are not even finishing their high school education. Between a boring, seemingly irrelevant curriculum and the breakdown of the family unit, it is becoming increasingly difficult to convince kids to stay in school. The trend is worsening, and statistics seem to be heading to the point at which half of all kids prematurely abandon the supposed lifeline to their future economic possibilities. If that weren't enough, schools are often rife with drugs and disciplinary issues. Public schools must either change or collapse. This shaking of the kingdom of education will be presenting unprecedented opportunities to Josephs who will dream the dreams of God.

The Lord is inviting His Josephs to jump into this fray with divine solutions that will revolutionize education. Our existing solution of creating private Christian schools hasn't been dramatically more effective than its public counterpart. Many Christian schools still hold some of the foundational errors of the public system—sometimes doing even more damage to their students in the name of God. There are good models among private Christian schools, but they can be as boring and as driven by human reason as public schools are. When they then top off their educational approach with the poison of legalistic Christianity, the result is a recipe for producing far less than what God has planned for us.

For example, consider that the primary eschatology taught to many of our children in many Christian schools is the hope of the Rapture. Is it any wonder that we have not been raising Josephs but rather robotic "sons of Leah"? Is it any wonder that according to some reports, more than half of Christian high school graduates lose their faith within a year of being in a mainline university? When you give instruction that primarily focuses on preparing students for death, that leaves a tremendous vacuum to be filled by those who will instruct them in what to do while they're still living. The good news here is that all of this is going to begin to change—in a hurry.

A TREASURE TROVE OF NEW JOSEPH SCHOOLS

Joseph schools are coming, and they will understand the kingdom of God and will teach and instruct from that foundation. These schools will focus on activating and interacting with the creative right side of the brain, thus breaking the stronghold of the "mind of reason" that currently leads to humanism in our educational institutions. These schools will offer such enjoyable instruction that many parents will sacrifice dearly to allow their children to learn in this environment. These schools will not operate as indoctrinators of Christianity but will offer a kingdom template that does acknowledge and interact with God. The curriculum will lead students to the water of Jesus without forcing them to drink. As a result, these schools will be very popular, even among non-Christians, and an entire franchise of these private schools will emerge in short order. Their foundational template will be the seven mountains of society and preparing kids to thrive in the head of society. I prophetically saw one school franchise being widely modeled, but there will be many other new models that will advance.

NEW PILOT PUBLIC SCHOOLS

Another way that the Lord will release His Josephs is by giving them unusual favor in certain public school settings. They will take many approaches and strategies from the private "Joseph schools" and incorporate them into pilot public school initiatives. These schools will so far outperform the traditional public schools that entire school systems will adapt these models. These schools will carry creative God-ideas that tackle the serious problems of rebellion and class disruption. Whatever the problem and challenge is, the Lord has practical, creative solutions. A Joseph will discover these solutions and receive God's favor to implement them.

A NEW, ANOINTED CURRICULUM

God has an entire treasure chest of divine curricula coming forth. In this treasure chest is a more exciting way of teaching and learning math, science, art, geography, and virtually everything that can be taught. It will be not just a more exciting way of teaching and learning; it will be an anointed way, because it will be sourced by the favor of God.

NEW SEVEN MOUNTAIN UNIVERSITIES

New universities will rise up almost overnight. Most of these will be hosted by major church ministries that will have great latitude and freedom in instructing people in the ways of the kingdom of God. These will be schools of the Holy Spirit that will connect very strongly with a rising generation of world changers who will burn with passion to see God made famous in all of the earth.

These universities will recruit, equip, train, and mobilize a forthcoming army through the grid and template of the seven mountains. Many of them will be so successful, so large, and so prosperous that the world will flock to them. The leaders of many future nations will receive instruction in these universities, and several will garner a worldwide reputation in a very short time. These will be the new Harvards, Yales, and Princetons, universities that were initially founded on Christian principles to train ministers—though the Lord will yet offer these institutions a chance to return to the original ideals of their founders.

As I am writing this, I am overtaken with how wondrous and revolutionary this will be. There is great joy in the heart of our God for modeling the instruction of heaven here on earth. As we do that, many will come, many will see, and many will put their trust in Him.

DISCOVERIES REFUTING THE FOUNDATIONS OF DARWINISM

The study of quantum physics and quantum mechanics—scientific principles related to matter and energy at atomic and subatomic levels—is about to send the scientific community into a collision with the Maker. Some suggest that this has already happened, but what I'm envisioning in particular is an unavoidable confrontation with the fact of intelligent design behind the entire universe. Scientists are about to peer into the quantum world to a degree that they will find a smiling God staring back at them. This will revolutionize the scientific community in general and will strengthen the foundational guidelines of all true education.

There have long been contradictory views not only between evolutionary thought and a biblical worldview, but also within each camp. The Lord will honor a Joseph with a discovery that will greatly clear up the riddle of it all. He has been setting up the scientific community for a great "aha" moment, and it will soon happen. God will greatly enjoy doing this, and we will greatly enjoy being His people as this is happening. Eye has not seen nor ear heard the wonders that He is preparing before us. He will reveal His glory in this and every other sector of society, and it will far surpass what we have been able even to dream about. The unseen world will soon be seen as never before, and we will all know we are gazing at that which is eternal. God is going to show off.

NEW DAYCARE SCHOOLS

Someone will get a God-dream and start a new kingdom daycare. This daycare will be a divine preschool that will set a very necessary foundation in the lives of the children. Because it will operate under childcare guidelines instead of school guidelines, its creators will have great latitude to make it as kingdom-oriented as desired. A pastor and his wife will quit their church and recognize this daycare as the "church" God wants them to run. (Others may do the same, but I see one couple leading the way.) The members of their church will assist them in making this their major mission field. An entire chain of these schools will be opened throughout this nation and then in other nations. This daycare will operate so professionally, with so much excellence, and with so much behavioral fruit in the children that parents will be begging that their children be allowed to attend. It will be a virtual all-day church meeting, but it will be done creatively and won't seem anything like a church meeting as we know it. Kids will sing and thank and praise God every day. They will bring prayer requests from home, and those prayers will be supernaturally met. This daycare approach will be so anointed that 90 percent of the kids who profess faith in Jesus during these days will stick to their confession throughout their life. Many parents will come to the Lord as this school assists them in their parenting. There will be a natural segue between this daycare model and the kingdom schools that the children graduate into.

SEVEN MOUNTAIN EVANGELISM

Get used to the term *seven mountain evangelism*. This phenomenon will explode upon us. I mentioned in the previous section how parents will come to the Lord as kingdom schools reach their children, but we'll see this dynamic in all mountains of society. God will attract people to Himself through the glory He reveals through His children in each sector of society. This will draw many more to the Lord than our intentional TV evangelism does. Even when successful, our mass media evangelism efforts generally net only converts, not disciples. God's ways are the real attraction for people. As we creatively model His ways, people will be drawn to Him. As He is showcased on the tops of the mountains, all nations will come running.

14

Joseph on the Mountain of Media

MY THOUGHTS ON the mountain of media are primarily about secular media outlets. Christian television programs are only loosely related to this mountain; they are primarily a ministry venture on the mountain of religion and have little impact on the way society approaches and perceives media.

The mountain of media is one of the most up-for-grabs sectors of society, mainly because existing foundational media have been rocked and are in a state of transition. Newspapers that have been staples of life for decades are going bankrupt, and new media outlets coming out of the technological revolution are rising up all over the world. Newspapers no longer offer the latest news; in this fast paced society, day-old news is virtually ancient. Newspapers will have to either reinvent themselves or come crashing down. Many of them already have more online readers than print readers.

In addition to the crisis of daily newspapers, the traditional TV news giants are teetering and shaking under the new media landscape. Part of that shaking has come from the removal of their collective masks; in many ways, some have been exposed as propaganda machines for liberal politics. Traditional news networks practically sang the Pledge of Allegiance to Barack Obama during the most recent election season while twisting most of what came out of the mouths of John McCain and, to a greater degree, Sarah Palin. The widespread perception that they have lost a sense of truth and objectivity has created ongoing opportunities for other media outlets to grow.

JOSEPHS AND NEW, CREDIBLE MEDIA

The Lord will greatly help Josephs arise on the mountain of media, especially in the years up to 2015. In general, the Joseph anointing is an anointing that meets needs in such a unique way that wealth is a natural byproduct. This will specifically be the case on the mountain of media. God is first awakening His Josephs and then inviting them to dream His dreams to displace darkness in the media. The world is tired of ongoing exposure to non-redemptive news. In recent history, media have served primarily to magnify fears and anxieties, and people's fear and anxiety levels are getting so out of control that they are choosing to change channels rather than subject themselves to such negativity. This creates a great opportunity for Josephs of media to arise with redemptive news reporting. There will continue to be very serious news to report, but it's possible to report such news and still fan the flames of hope. News outlets that carry a spirit of good news will be in such high demand that the ratings of these outlets will dramatically rise in the coming years.

JOSEPH NEWSPAPERS

I believe a Joseph-operated newspaper will go national and within a very short period of time become the newspaper of most national credibility. It will carry daily news and sports, but its reporting of time-sensitive news will be peripheral; it will be carried by the power and anointing of its columnists and editorial angles. It will feature rising voices that are able to speak to the nation at key times. The voice of God will speak through this newspaper, giving the perfect balance of hope, truth, and reality checks. Rather than majoring in fear-mongering, conspiracy-laced, old-school conservatism, it will steer the nation in areas of needed repentance. Its fresh voices will be known for their humor, creativity of expression, and incisive wisdom. These voices will be Joseph voices who recognize the times and discern what needs to be done. They won't be hand-wringers, crying wolf at every turn. In fact, they will so rarely cry wolf that when they actually do so, their warning will carry great weight. People will trust their objectivity, and ongoing exposure to their instruction will lead many to the Lord—not by direct evangelistic appeals but by their promotion of proper values, which will lead people to desire a proper relationship with God. This will be the mountain of media's version of seven mountain evangelism.

JOSEPH TV CHANNELS

God will give Josephs favor to dismantle the influence of the spirit of Apollyon, the spirit that illegally dominates the mountain of media. In much the same way that God will raise up voices in the press, so will He favor His sons and daughters to present these credible voices to the people. People will have a desperate hunger to know what's really going on as we shift full-throttle into the perils and adventures of the Last Days. They will constantly be asking, "Is this something we should fear, or is everything OK?" A significant assignment for media Josephs will be, as part of their journalistic homework, to never just state a hopeless piece of news. They will have found the key people or ideas to respond to the crisis. These new Joseph journalists will consider the reporting work undone unless a "hope clause" is revealed in their report.

This will be a very profound but stealthy way to reveal the kingdom in these coming days. God's solutions for impossible situations will be discovered journalistically and appropriately declared as credible news stories. The result for media Josephs will be high ratings and high subscriptions—a financial aspect to the success on this mountain. That won't be the purpose, of course, but it will be the effect. Not everything that Christians try to do in the media will prosper—after all, there are already plenty of "Leah's sons" in this profession—but everything that Josephs do will eventually prosper. As I've pointed out in earlier chapters, God will place a coat of many colors only on His Josephs, even though He loves His other children, too. The coat of many colors is a mantle of favor that receives the dreams of God and displaces the enemy. The kingdom of God always comes "not by might, nor by power, but by His Spirit" (Zech. 4:6, author's paraphrase).

INTERNET JOSEPHS

A multitude of media Josephs can operate Internet news sites, but a very respected Internet news source will be owned and operated by a Joseph who understands his or her mission and will do it so well that the site will receive millions of hits every day. There will also be a Joseph blog that combines such humor and wit with its message that it will receive millions of daily visits. It will be 100 percent kingdom-motivated, but almost no one will know that because of the stealth package its kingdom message is wrapped in.

I see media Josephs arising like ants all over the Internet in all kinds of stealth poses, but they will know what their mission is and will be so highly favored that hundreds of thousands and even millions listen. A kingdom chorus will come out of the godly invasion taking place through the Internet and other instant communications outlets. There are already media Josephs who don't recognize themselves as such but who are operating through media venues like blogs and Facebook and YouTube. The better they recognize their call and mission, the more favor they will receive to displace distorted news from the media mountain. This is an extremely important mission field in which a communication anointing can quickly make room for itself.

JOSEPH MAGAZINES

Josephs will develop and run many new creative magazines. These publications will be birthed from God-dreams and will become very popular very quickly, and they won't be the obvious Christian magazines we all know about already. One will be a magazine that reports on the lives of the rich and famous—not to gossip about them but to promote their charitable acts all over the world. It will stealthily give glory to God. It will provoke people to good works by exalting generosity and charity, never straying into rumormongering or tabloid journalism but remaining true to its kingdom underpinnings. This positive publicity will engender competition among the rich and famous to be recognized for doing good. They will want to be mentioned in it.

A secular magazine on dream interpretation will provide prophetic direction for a lost generation. An accompanying Web site will provide live chatting for dream interpretation. Not only will this instruct people about dreams, but it will also reveal Christ in some most marvelous ways. It will be a tool for salvation, for destiny, for hope, and for meeting all kinds of needs.

I see a variety of magazines exploding forth that address matters on all seven mountains of society. God will be coming out of the box in many of these, and many good church people (a.k.a. Leah's sons) won't get it. God will release an amazing creative genius through the dreams He gives His Josephs.

JOSEPHS ON THE RADIO

There will be no media outlet in which Josephs can't make an appearance in God's favor. College-aged Josephs will begin to take over radio stations all over the place—either directly or through amazingly creative ideas they will receive for very successful, never-thought-of-before programming. There is still a bright future in radio, and, in fact, the Josephs in radio will cause a revival in radio listenership. So much adventure and godly fruit can be found through this medium, and God is eager to showcase them.

THE SHORT SHELF LIFE OF MEDIA LIES

By 2015, God's media Josephs will have so invaded every sector of media that lies and distortions will have a very short shelf life. This will be a very important element in the invasion of all seven mountains; the enemy must not be able to misrepresent what's taking place. The mountain of government cannot ultimately be secured apart from a sustained presence of God's children on the mountain of media.

Conspiratorial political organizations already know this and advance strategically with this reality in mind. The Joseph movement will not be conspiratorial, but it will understand the realities of mountain living. It will recognize that if government is the brain, then media is the mouth. What comes out of the mouth has a powerful effect on the brain. Sarah Palin, for example, did not lack political expertise in the 2008 election. She lacked the ability to neutralize lies, half-truths, and distortions coming from the media. She was isolated because she was a pioneer. Soon, however, all mountains will be filled with an army of God. It will be Joel's army, and they *will* destroy the works of Satan. That task goes well beyond saving souls. Satan's works will be destroyed as he is evicted from the seven mountains at the head of society.

15

Joseph on the Mountain of Economy

ONE OF THE biblical meanings of *glory* is "wealth." When Scripture says that "the whole earth is filled with His glory," it also means that God's resources are everywhere. I've indicated that He will be making available one quadrillion dollars of His loot for His Josephs during this seven-year period. This is not for the purposes of producing artificial wealth—for example, manipulating Wall Street with bogus trades that are too good to be true. This is clear-cut, heaven-sent treasure. And, as I've emphasized, this is not simply for the sake of lining Christians' pockets with money. Josephs are kingdom-focused, not self-focused. God is righteously rich, and He is going to enjoy showing off His abundance over the next several years by putting His resources in the right hands. He's looking for favorite sons and daughters to partner with.

Once Joseph's plan was implemented, his abundance became too much to calculate. We read in Genesis 41:49, "Joseph gathered very much grain, as the sand of the sea, until he stopped counting, for it was immeasurable." One "Joseph plan" accessed an immeasurable amount of treasure. He was counting, but he had to stop because there were just too many zeros in that number. That's my God.

The mountain of economy or business seems to be one of the likeliest arenas for a Joseph to show up. We have almost infinite ways in which we can go after God's hidden treasures on this mountain. I will share some things I feel God has revealed to me, but God will be showing His Josephs many, many other ideas and trends.

NEW FORMS OF ENERGY

Foreseeing the discovery of new forms of energy doesn't require a lot of prophetic ability because it's being widely attempted and speculated about even in secular society. But I believe a new energy philosophy will engender the discovery of new energy resources. It will be a parabolic reflection on the transfer of wealth that will be taking place. Whereas man has been looking underground for that which is black, we will now begin to look to heaven's resources for energy and wealth. We have long leaned on coal and oil as the world's primary sources of energy. The way this has functioned reveals significantly that the spirit of Mammon is orchestrating things behind the scenes. Though all earthly resources are a blessing from God, it's interesting to note the strong connection between nations rich in oil and the Islamic religion. Many in Islamic nations believe that this "blessing of Allah" is significant proof that they are the chosen people of earth, a belief that has served in their self-delusion. Mammon has been clearly at work monetarily propping up societies that are the most anti-Israel and anti-Christ. Much of the funding of terrorism comes almost directly from the resources of oil. It really has been a "black gold." By 2015, we will see that God has totally undermined the financing of Islam—not in order to judge Muslims but in order to win them over en masse. The loss of oil revenue will play a significant part in removing the veil from the Muslim world. God will passionately go after them, and He is starting by destroying their false gods.

Not only will there be a coming transfer of wealth, but there will also be a transfer of the source of wealth. Joseph dreams and ideas will come from above, and then in practical ways we will see breakthroughs in the energy sources that come from above, all of which are parabolic expressions of who God is—the sun, water, and wind. While underground black sources of energy pollute the earth, all the heavenly sources of energy are the kind that don't. That's highly symbolic.

This doesn't mean all Christians need to immediately get out of the oil business (though do pay attention to any promptings of the Lord). This trend toward heavenly energy sources will develop over some time, though probably quicker than many imagine. Solar energy is already well known, but a technological breakthrough will simplify and economize the process of how it is accessed. In some ways, this breakthrough will override foundational assumptions about the process. Expect a Joseph dreamer to have an impact in this breakthrough.

Wind energy is also well known, but new breakthroughs will harness wind in entirely new ways. Some of you who have been working on this are about to receive dreams from God that will give you the breakthrough you have been looking for. I'm seeing a wind energy that doesn't rely on fan concepts. It's possible that this discovery will already be made by the time this is published.

Water has long been a valuable energy source, but gigantic breakthroughs in how to harness it are coming. I believe at least three viable sources of energy will come from water. Perhaps the most significant will have to do with activating water's hydrogen element and the ability to harness it economically. This will be different than the principle on which hydrogen cars run. While in Jerusalem last year, I saw a vision that had to do with sound activating hydrogen. A certain sonar frequency will cause hydrogen to come alive in just the right way.

An Alternative Stock Market

I have seen that by 2015 we will have an alternative stock market functioning on entirely different values. These will be kingdom values—the stocks in this market will have a utility value other than producing capital. Though Bernie Madoff has been marginalized as an unusual Wall Street figure, the truth is that most of the underpinnings of Wall Street comprise a virtual Ponzi scheme. Bernie obviously had zero product utility, yet much of Wall Street has been proven to have a similarly low actual product utility. Money has been artificially created by the horizontal trading of paper. Imagine, for example, ten people sitting around a table. The first one sells a can of soda to the second person for $1. Then the second person sells the same can to the next for $2, and so forth around the table. Because of the multiple transactions, the tenth person eventually holds a can of soda valued at $10, yet it's the same $1 can. Person number one can get the sodas straight from the factory, and they are now somehow worth $10 each to him because of around-the-table transactions. He is suddenly ten times richer based solely on trades. This transactional wealth is artificial, not sustainable, real wealth. It can therefore disappear almost overnight when markets crash.

When the value of what you own is only on paper and depends entirely on people's beliefs, then a crisis of faith (ironically) can cause "belief" to disappear, which causes wealth to disappear along with it. Perceived wealth *is* wealth—but only for a season.

Economies and stock markets will always involve some element of faith, but markets must be set up under a different set of values so they won't collapse. An alternative stock market that doesn't operate from a foundation of capitalism will be set up. When capitalism is the stated foundation of operation, those who buy into that operation are officially serving Mammon (greed), because the bottom line is capital. But a stock market that has a different bottom line will come about. The bottom line will reflect values of viability that extend beyond capital. Products will necessarily have a socially redeeming quality to them. This market will be run on the Joseph principle: meet a need in such a unique way that wealth is the byproduct.

This new stock market(s) will be intentionally firewalled from the rest of the economy so as not to be subject to the domino effect of collapsing systems. One reason the whole world has experienced an economic crisis is that everything is connected to everything (the interdependence of globalism), and one economic virus can spread rapidly. We need to use some of the wisdom of computer virus protection plans and apply them to the economy. This will happen.

The Joseph Test for Businesses

The first mark of a Joseph business is that it is uniquely meeting a need. The second mark is that wealth is the byproduct, not the goal. These will be your important diagnostic tests for the future if you are looking to have a business that God will put His mantle of favor on. The coming Josephs will be about uniquely meeting needs. God's dreams will come to you as you posture yourself before Him for this purpose. Discover an area of your primary passion that goes beyond making money. Making money as a primary passion is clear evidence of a stronghold of Mammon.

For example, I've seen that there will be new neighborhood developments based on a Joseph's passion to inspire community-mindedness. Wealth will be a byproduct of these developments. One can build houses motivated solely by the possibility of capital gains or by the desire to meet needs. This principle applies everywhere on the business/economy mountain. Know that God will not endorse those endeavors that are driven by the bottom line, even if those endeavors momentarily succeed.

GREAT MEDICAL BREAKTHROUGHS

God will release Joseph dreams to His children that will engender great medical breakthroughs. These dreams are available for those who will get closer to Him. Cancer and AIDS will ultimately bow both to the healing power of God and to the biotechnological power of God. In more ways than we know, these things are actually very connected. We will be getting God's power to *see* correctively into the bloodstream at about the same time an abundance of healings are being reported in crusades and the like. A real joining of God and science will soon come because science is headed on a collision course with the very God of the universe many scientists have denied. When they crash into the God-atom, the subatomic particle that carries His voice, a seismic shift that connects science and God will lead to the unraveling of many medical mysteries. In the future, there will not be a credible scientist who does *not* believe in God. He will be staring at us and speaking to us at every quantum turn. He will be an unavoidable reality—and will enjoy this a lot.

Just as sonar frequencies will be instrumental in harnessing energy, remarkable healing properties will be discovered by "cranking the volume" on certain elements. The sound of blood will be proven to have powerful healing qualities, and those who can magnify and reproduce that sound will make headlines. This will be a parabolic message as well as a practical breakthrough. Don't be too attached to your technologies, as they will change in unprecedented fashion. Your financial future won't be based on the technology you hold but on the Dreamgiver you have access to.

NEW JOSEPH WEAPONS OF WAR?

If the idea of Joseph weapons shakes you up, just remember that the greatest peacemaker on earth is often overwhelming power. The dreams of God are about to invade the weapons divisions of the United States and Israel. A new "bomb" will atomically defuse nuclear bombs. There will be great technological advances in weapons of *defense* at all levels. God will give Josephs dreams and ideas for countermeasures against every means of destruction that exists. Israel will have a sonar weapon that will be God's *shofar* (trumpet) over them and for them. It will disarm and penetrate virtually everything. There will be no defense against this weapon; it will therefore be a great peacemaker.

New Financing Structures

An entirely new way of doing business and banking is coming. New infrastructural rules that follow Joseph guidelines of unique utility will be implemented. Banking institutions will provide credit counseling as part of their initial relationship with new customers; their stated goals will involve healing the financially sick. These banks will seek the financial restoration of families. As they look out for the prosperity of others, they will prosper themselves. They will not do business based on credit scores alone but will implement relational dynamics in their practices.

God will manifest His kingdom in many different ways in every conceivable sector of the business world. He wants the kingdom way of doing things modeled through His Josephs everywhere. He can prosper you in *any* sector of society you operate out of as a byproduct of the kingdom service you are doing. Just get out of your box!

Redefining *Prosperity*

God may have to help some of us redefine what prosperity is. It has little to do with having a specific number of zeros in our bank account. It isn't about the number of toys we possess. It is not the size of our 401(k). Prosperity is a spiritual place in which we know that God is taking care of us and that He will continue to do so. It's where we know Him as Jehovah-jireh—"the Lord who *is* provision."

We don't know that Joseph ever had a bank account or many possessions; yet he was greatly prospered by God. He had an inexhaustible Most High trust fund. He prospered among the flock, he prospered with Midianite merchants, he prospered as a servant in Potiphar's house, he prospered in prison, and he prospered over all of Egypt. He prospered because "he was a successful man" (Gen. 39:2). Sometimes he had irons around his legs, and sometimes he had a golden chain around his neck; but he was always prosperous. Prosperity is a position of knowing that God is providing whatever you need at that stage of your life. It is recognizable favor that translates differently depending on God's stages of process with you and His assignment over your life. In the final stage of prosperity, He will cause you to be a channel of prosperity for many others and even for entire nations.

God wants us to manifest prosperity in every sector of society, so let's do it well. The day you lose your fear about whether God will continue to take care of you is the day you become prosperous. That is, of course, assuming you are a Joseph who is earnestly pursuing intimacy and relationship with God. A presumptuous, lazy fearlessness will leave you in the poor house. Leah's sons were going to starve, not based on the weakness of their economic situation (they managed and owned more than Joseph, who was only the steward of another's wealth) but based on the weakness of their relational situation. All marvelous things that God will do in the latter days will flow out of the personal romance of God and someone. He really is the rewarder of those who diligently seek Him (Heb. 11:6). The great reward is Himself, but other observable rewards come with Him. Provision is not just something He does but someone He is. Creativity is also not just something He gives but someone He is. And authority, too, is not just something He gives but someone He is. He offers Himself to His children.

Rise up, Josephs! First invade the heart of the Dreamgiver, then get and take His dreams and make Him famous in all the earth!

16

Joseph on the Mountain of Family

THE MOUNTAIN OF religion is known for traditional ministries that aim to reach families and meet their spiritual needs. While it's possible to have a family ministry far-reaching enough to impact this mountain, this generally doesn't happen. The mountain of family is distinct from the mountain of religion. It's where we target social structures and bring the kingdom of God to them. Government agencies and programs like the Department of Family and Children Services (DFACS) and welfare, as well as family law coming out of the judicial branch of government, are examples of measures that address the mountain of family. There is plenty of room on this mountain to create new institutions that will be successful in healing marriages, families, and individuals—institutions that don't require a tithe and ritual attendance before people can encounter the Lord.

This entire mountain is a pool of ministry just waiting for someone to come jump in. The Josephs who will position themselves on the mountain of family will receive an abundance of dreams from God. While many people are striving to find a place of ministry behind a pulpit, screaming opportunities are being ignored simply because we have not recognized the harvest field that exists. Following are some of the places some new Josephs will arise with a powerful mantle of favor.

BABYSITTING SERVICE

A Joseph will arise and recognize this field of ministry and develop a national babysitting service that functions with the specific mission of meeting the unique needs of families. Those who run it will be pastors at heart, as will all of their employees. Even though many employees will be youths, they will be expected to understand that they are functioning in a pastoral calling. They will develop different ministry plans for the homes in which they serve based on the ages of the children and the amount of time the service spends there. In every case, "babysitters" will at least pray for the household and its children while they serve. The babysitters will also recommend books and materials for parents based on recognized areas of need. Through this ministry, families will be seen as an important mission field. I see this ministry being financially subsidized by people with great resources in order to keep the babysitting service economical for families. Babysitters will be on a salary of sorts, and the babysitting fees that families pay will help offset expenses without entirely funding the ministry.

DAYCARE CENTERS

The daycare centers I mentioned in chapter 13, "Joseph on the Mountain of Education," will just as powerfully impact the mountain of family. The Lord will raise up Josephs who will uniquely manifest the kingdom of God in these two sectors of society simultaneously.

ALTERNATIVE DFACS

I believe it's the will of God for His kingdom-minded children to invade the entire Department of Family and Children Services (DFACS) and reform and restructure this key agency. Many who are called to be pastors may need to consider "pastoring" on this mountain and not in a formal church. Women pastors who have faced the scarcity of opportunities in traditional church roles may find fulfilling and fruitful options to take their place and shine with God's heart in this field.

Having said that, I also see a ministry that works closely with DFACS and is sanctioned by DFACS to help with very difficult family situations. It will be as if DFACS is sub-contracting their most difficult cases because of the tremendous fruit of restoration by this organization. I envision this ministry/organization as the alternative DFACS, as it will function officially as an extension of DFACS. The purpose of this ministry will not be to proselytize but to bring healing to families. This will allow it to not be singled out as an attempt to indoctrinate religious beliefs, but it will bring people to God because of its ability to restore families.

FOSTER FAMILY STRATEGIES

Josephs will arise and rally the body of Christ around the cause of foster families. Many families will see it as their ministry to be a place of refuge for the wounded and rejected. The Christian community has been a little hypocritical in the past by being horrified over abortion but not stepping up to the plate in reaching out to living "aborted" children—those who have been rejected or lost after birth. Most foster children are walking abortees, but many Christians haven't seen the pastoral opportunity this represents. Many couples with a pastoral heart will understand that they are called to pastor through offering themselves as foster parents.

FREE LEGAL HELP FOR DIVORCE

I see another Joseph arising to offer free legal help for people who want to get divorced. In order for a couple to qualify for a free divorce, however, they will be required by this legal association to undergo a month of free marital counseling. The initial goal, of course, will be to save the marriage if it's salvageable and not an abusive situation. In some cases, this organization will have to provide the free divorce it promised, but it will at least have had a chance at saving the marriage. It will be funded by outside sources because it exists not to make money but to heal families in any and every stage of marital conflict.

JOSEPH JUDGES

As Josephs continue to arise and awake, the Lord will begin to position them at every conceivable legal juncture related to families. The available mantle is such a real anointing from God that I can see a day when our entire Supreme Court is made up of Josephs—people raised up by God to impact families with godly wisdom. If you have already been dreaming of this, get ready. God is going to do through the mountain of family what we haven't been able to accomplish through elections. As I was writing this, I saw a vision of nine mantles being held out by the Lord, each one designed for someone assigned to the Supreme Court. Impossible? Of course. But that's who He is, the God of the impossible. This is a very small thing for Him. He searches for those He can strongly promote in this way. "The eyes of the LORD run to and fro throughout the whole earth, to show Himself strong on behalf of those whose heart is loyal to Him" (2 Chron. 16:9).

You don't have to wonder if God would want to do this kind of thing. His eyes run throughout the whole earth just looking for those who will defy the odds and believe for "crazy" stuff. The verse before that promise proves that He's capable of tackling impossible situations: "Were the Ethiopians and the Lubim not a huge army with very many chariots and horsemen? Yet, because you relied on the LORD, He delivered them into your hand" (2 Chron. 16:8). Your crazy stuff is His average, easy work. He loves slaying giants with very small stones. Let Him pick you up out of His stream of relationship and watch Him catapult you into the head of a Goliath. Nothing gives Him greater pleasure. He really enjoys doing this.

The Last Great Work

> Behold, I will send you Elijah the prophet before the coming of the great and dreadful day of the LORD. And he will turn the hearts of the fathers to the children, and the hearts of the children to their fathers, lest I come and strike the earth with a curse.
>
> —MALACHI 4:5–6

These are the last two verses of the Old Testament. After they were recorded, Scripture was silent for the next four hundred years. These verses tell us that the last great work God will do before He returns is restoring families. If this were not to happen, He says, He would have to annihilate the earth with a curse. Why? Because the foundation of His plan begins with family and its proper operation. Since this is such a primary focus of "the eyes of the Lord," we can be assured that this is an area where we will be wonderfully helped as we engage the giants before us.

17

Joseph on the Mountain of Celebration

GOD IS GOING to showcase the inexhaustible supremacy of His creativity on the mountain of celebration. When we really understand that his eyes are running through the whole earth, looking to see who gets what He is doing, then we will begin accessing portions of our never-before-seen inheritance.

TREASURE TROVE OF MOVIES

I saw in a vision that the Lord has a whole treasure trove of golden movies available for His sons and daughters to access. This treasure trove contains some of the best stories ever told to humanity. There are epic stories of incredible adventure, romance, danger, and mystery—but all told from heaven's standpoint and with heaven's purposes. The eyes of the Lord will begin to find those who are coming into Him and discovering the treasures of His heart. The world cannot compete with the stories that will begin to be downloaded by His Josephs on this mountain. This is the mountain where He will really show off. This is the mountain where He will release amazing glory.

I have also seen in a vision a packed cinema in which, at some point in the movie, the entire crowd gets down on their knees and begins to sob as they are gripped by the glory on the movie. In the future, movies will carry glory, and those that carry the most glory will also generally make the most money. I see a coming day in which the five greatest-grossing movies of all time are specifically produced by someone wearing a Joseph mantle. Maybe if I had greater faith I could see further into the future than that, but that's a good start.

We have to realize that God is not going to come judge the world "in fire and brimstone" because He just couldn't compete with Satan's products. It's true that He will come in with some purifying judgments, but He is also going to show up Satan on the tops of every mountain of society. He is going to cause love to triumph in every visible sector of culture. The knowledge of the glory of the Lord filling the earth goes beyond His judgments. The glory of who He is will ultimately triumph on all the mountains. Satan's great resistance has not held Him back from doing so. He has held back because He has been waiting on Josephs on whom He could place many-colored mantles. When He gets those Josephs, the satanic resistance will be as difficult as hot butter is to a knife. The *great* battle was already fought. Jesus did that one by Himself. He has already reclaimed all legal power and authority on earth. All other power has already been defeated and therefore operates illegally. God now only searches for those close enough to His heart to enforce what has already been won.

Once Joel's army starts marching, everything dissipates in front of it.

> A people come, great and strong, the like of whom has never been....Their appearance is like the appearance of horses; and like swift steeds, so they run. With a noise like chariots *over mountaintops* they leap, like the noise of a flaming fire that devours the stubble, like a strong people set in battle array....They run like mighty men, they climb the wall like men of war; every one marches in formation, and they do not break ranks. They do not push one another; every one marches in his own column....The LORD gives voice before His army, for His camp is very great.
>
> —JOEL 2:2, 4–5, 7–8, 11, EMPHASIS ADDED

Some believe that this "Joel's army" is in fact the enemy that God is using. The intensity of this army's demeanor and its destructiveness has led to this arguable but, in my opinion, erroneous conclusion. Verse 11 calls them "His army," and though God was known to use an evil army as His army at times, I believe this passage speaks of God's people, teamed up with angels. In its original prophetic message, this passage speaks of events that have already transpired; but it has a powerful secondary prophetic application for us today.

We are here not just to garner decisions for Christ. We have a mission to destroy the works of Satan. A "vicious" army of God is in fact now arising, and it will mean business in a way that no army ever has. We will invade every sector of our promised land, and we will be ruthless with spiritual forces of darkness everywhere we go. People will never be the target of this ruthlessness; only the darkness that has held people captive has need to fear. This is war, and it's going to be an enjoyable war. His kingdom always comes in joy as it is being established.

KINGDOM REALITY SHOWS

There will be an avalanche of new kingdom-oriented reality shows that will be great hits. The world wants authenticity; that's why reality shows have been popular, even though many of them are mostly staged. Some Josephs in the television industry will create shows that are closer to reality and will stealthily release the kingdom of God by showcasing God in unique ways. The world cannot compete with the creativity that is now available for His sons and daughters who want to carry His glory.

MUSICAL TREASURES

God has a musical treasure chest available for His people. From what I can tell, not even one of these treasures has been discovered yet. Even with all the good Christian music out there, there are still sounds to be heard that come right from the heartbeat of God. These sounds will be discovered by those who sit in His presence—not through horizontal expression that merely edifies listeners but through vertical exploration into the burning coals of His heart. This music will blow the world away.

People are limited from seeing the center of God's heart because they haven't had the faith or vision to believe what they see. They aren't accessing the exuberance of heaven because of bad eschatology—a lack of prophetic vision. Where there is no prophetic vision, people meander and undersell God, even when they are intimate with Him. If you go to God for His music while believing that the only hope for this world is the Rapture followed by judgment, you won't be able to hear the sounds and music of His heart. Some things can only be heard when you see His glorious arising through His sons and daughters.

Many Josephs will awaken and begin to find the hidden treasure in the field of God's heart. This will carry glory within the four walls of the church, but it will also bring glory to displace the darkness on this mountain, where His creativity is celebrated. The coming sounds of heaven will rock the earth. In fact, the sounds of heaven will always accompany the initial establishing of new things on earth, just as on the day of Pentecost, when the sound of heaven brought in the new power the church would operate in.

> When the Day of Pentecost had fully come, they were all with one accord in one place. And suddenly there came a *sound from heaven*, as of a rushing mighty wind, and it filled the whole house where they were sitting.
>
> —ACTS 2:1–2, EMPHASIS ADDED

A sound of heaven that will invigorate an entire generation is about to come to earth. This time it won't be just for the church but for God's entire creation. Creation will shake with this new sound because it will tell the world that the new measure of mighty wind is here. When Peter said on Pentecost, "This is what was spoken of by the prophet Joel," and that God would pour out His Spirit on all flesh (Acts 2:16–17), he was talking about a sound of heaven. When God pours out something new of His Spirit on His sons and daughters, it first comes in a sound. These coming sounds will be for "all flesh." Joseph people will be able to add lyrics to them, and they will be released through professionally mixed CDs. But professional mixing is not the key, and we must be careful not to overly tinker with the sound of heaven. The professionalism of it all will be the wrapping paper, but the sound itself is what will cause the earth to shake.

This will be important to remember in all areas of society. Manifesting the kingdom of God is not about manifesting human excellence. The kingdom of God comes in excellence, but it is an excellence that supersedes what humans can produce. The top level of excellence that the world can produce is still only human glory, which is humanism. The glory of our Creator is in another dimension, and it carries the *it* factor that the nations crave. We don't want to display His excellence sloppily, but we really must understand that He provides the elements that are difference-makers for shining in the darkness. Your horizontal diligence and effort can make you equal with the world, but your vertical diligence and effort are what garner you the Joseph mantle that no one can compete with.

THE NEW JOSEPH STYLE

I believe a new fashion will recover and restore the glory of the rainbow colors. The vision I saw was a Joseph mantle of the colors of the rainbow. The enemy has attempted to denigrate the glory of the rainbow and its colors by associating it with the homosexual movement and other fringe movements. The rainbow is a visual expression of God's glory. Revelation 4:3 tells us that there is a rainbow around the throne. This is not incidental symbolism; there is something important in recovering the glory of the rainbow. God will raise up a Joseph who will create a "rainbow wear" with God's favor on it to go worldwide. A generation of "rainbow children" will testify with their clothes of the glory and sovereignty of our God.

A NEW FELLOWSHIP OF CHRISTIAN ATHLETES

A new seven mountain paradigm will be grafted into the Fellowship of Christian Athletes and give it new life and anointing. This will equip athletes as never before to understand their platform and ministry. This understanding of identity and mission will bring about a profound shift in this movement, and athletes will begin to function as an army on the mountain of celebration. God will ignite this organization to bring great glory to His name. The Fellowship of Christian Athletes will become a battalion of Christian athletes. Off-field joint efforts will be even more exciting to athletes than their on-field efforts. Yet they will be driven to even greater on-field success so that the off-field events will shine brighter.

All the above are only tastes of what God has in mind for the mountain of celebration. This is where the glory of His creativity is specifically made to shine. He has mantles available in every sector of creative expression, and He is looking for sons and daughters after His heart.

> I pray that the eyes of your heart may be enlightened, so that you will know what is the hope of His calling, what are the riches of *the glory of His inheritance in the saints,* and what is the surpassing greatness of His power *toward us who believe.*
> —EPHESIANS 1:18–19, NAS, EMPHASIS ADDED

Before Jesus returns, He will showcase the glory of His inheritance in His saints. He makes surpassing greatness of power available for those who will believe that He wants to do this. Jesus manifesting in His children is the next great show on planet earth. Christ in you is the hope of glory (Col. 1:27). He wants the world to see what He looks like coming out of us.

18

Joseph on the Mountain of Religion

THERE WILL BE an explosion of new seven mountain churches across the earth. These "7M churches" will be those that have most perfectly understood the Great Commission, "Go therefore and make disciples of all the nations" (Matt. 28:19). For centuries, this has been the missional cry from the advancing church. In following this commission, many have attempted only to make converts of people in all nations. Others who have observed the long-term fruit of and emphasis on conversions alone have realized that the Great Commission was about making disciples, not just getting converts. Because Christianity must go beyond mere decisions and into lifestyle change, this will be an important new emphasis and adjustment. The 7M emphasis is awakening to the reality that the Great Commission is not just about discipling all people but all *nations*. It is a template, a faith, and a strategy for discipling not just the people of the nations but the nations themselves.

This upgrade in vision requires an overhaul in faith that can only come from getting inside God's heart and hearing how it beats for the nations. The Father invited Jesus to ask Him for the nations as an inheritance (Ps. 2:8), and multiple Scripture passages confirm that all nations will one day serve Him. For example, "All the ends of the world shall remember and turn to the LORD, and all the families of the nations shall worship before You" (Ps. 22:27).

What if we were actually supposed to believe that? He looks at the nations as families to be brought into Him.

PEOPLE GROUPS OR COUNTRIES?

I want to address a theological matter regarding the nations, because it directly affects which Great Commission you accept as your marching orders. The Greek word for "nation" and "people group" is *ethnos* (from which we get our word *ethnic*). Based on this premise, many have defined the Great Commission as targeting ethnic groups rather than nations. Though there is some validity in seeing *ethnos* as "people groups," I want to suggest that we are to see this word in the context of countries, too.

Jesus told of a coming day when He will gather all nations.

> All the nations will be gathered before Him, and He will separate them one from another, as a shepherd divides his sheep from the goats. And He will set the sheep on His right hand, but the goats on the left.
>
> —MATTHEW 25:32–33

The parable then goes on to explain that God will judge entire nations based on their righteous works (primarily of compassion) and will separate them into sheep nations and goat nations. I think the context here is pretty evident that He is not just going to be separating them into people groups but into politically defined nations. The coming judgment or blessing for them would clearly come based on how the nation in which they lived manifested righteousness.

The scriptures were never attempting to make some kind of special designations with its use of the word *ethnos*. Therefore, we need to stop doing that also. At the time in which Jesus was speaking, ethnic people groups were also nations, and nations were largely structured around ethnic groups. He wants them all, but in that process entire nations can be reached and discipled. Yes, every ethnic group that exists can and will be penetrated by the kingdom of God, but the latter-day separation of nations will be based on how they exhibited righteousness as a politically delineated entity. Accountability is determined based on how official structures administered righteousness and justice.

153 SHEEP NATIONS?

We must admit that the outworking of the End Times is laced with mystery. There have already been hundreds of misapplications and misreadings of how things will play out. The testimony of Scripture itself is that the prophecy experts, the Pharisees, completely failed to recognize Jesus when He showed up. Natural studies of prophetic scriptures clearly don't make someone an expert in eschatology. That was demonstrably the case in Jesus' day, and it remains the same for us today. Prophecy experts have been confidently predicting the future on TV and in books for the last several decades, even though they have consistently been proven wrong in assumption after assumption. That's because their "expertise" is based on a completely wrong philosophical premise. Even though this premise has been wrong for years, new generations of believers arise who don't know what the experts were saying a decade ago, so they continue to buy into the "new," revised prophetic perspectives. (I'm being vague because I don't want to specifically denigrate anyone.) The point is that there is a lot of End Times speculation making the rounds as revelation. Before it's over, we will know who has been mixing the most speculation with actual revelation. But for now, we should maintain enough humility to acknowledge that we all "know in part" and "prophesy in part" (1 Cor. 13:9).

That said, I believe that there is scriptural evidence that the Lord wants us to have faith for at least 153 countries to turn to Him at a national level and become "sheep nations." I will lay out the case for this from John 21, but let me emphasize that I realize that this interpretation has nothing to do with the original contextual meaning of this passage. I see this as one of Scripture's hidden mysteries to be uncovered specifically for this time. It's a prophetic interpretation of a text with another primary meaning. This must be considered an "in part" revelation.

In John 21, the last chapter of the gospel, Jesus shows Himself to His disciples for the third time after He was raised from the dead. Peter, John, James, and four other disciples had been fishing all night but had caught nothing. Seven disciples, some of them professional fishermen, couldn't even catch a single fish after trying all night. The fact that there were seven could point to this time when we have a seven mountain focus on the nations. While the dawn was coming upon the disciples, Jesus stood upon the shore

(v. 4), but it was still so dark that they didn't recognize Him. They were pretty close to Jesus—only two hundred cubits away (v. 8)—but couldn't see Him because He hadn't fully revealed Himself. Jesus called out to them and asked if they had caught any fish yet, and they told Him no, as if they were talking to anyone. This was the risen Lord, who now had all authority in heaven and earth, but they couldn't recognize His voice.

Jesus then instructed His disciples to cast the net on the right side, where they would find some fish. They obeyed and were amazed at the multitude of large fish—153 of them (John 21:11)—they hauled in and dragged to shore. John immediately recognized that it was the Lord who had been on shore speaking to them. "It is the Lord!" he said (v. 7). It was still too dark to see Jesus physically, but the incredible harvest let John know that this had to be the Lord. We know that because "when Simon Peter heard that it was the Lord," he plunged into the sea and started swimming to Jesus because they were close to shore (v. 7). This is an important detail of the story. It was the intimate disciple, John, who recognized the voice of the Lord, who had just told them how to catch the 153 large fish, but Jesus had not yet appeared in a visibly recognizable way. He was close to visibly appearing but hadn't done so yet.

This has eschatological implications. It points to how Josephs will fulfill the Great Commission. A group of disciples will go fishing for nations using the seven mountain template. It will be dark when they start, and they will work at this for a night season. As the dawn arises and as the "morning star" is about to reveal Himself (2 Pet. 1:19), there will be a command to cast the net to catch countries destined to be "sheep nations." We will be very close to Jesus at this time and very close to a new day, but neither will have been fully upon us. It will still take discernment to see Him and to recognize His voice. Those who recognize His voice will be in for a most amazing catch—153 "large fish" nations caught in the kingdom net they have laid out. The harvest will be so large that they will wonder if their nets will hold, but they will. They will drag the nations onto shore, and that's when the dawn will fully manifest with Jesus and the new age upon us.

I want to point out again that the sheep nations are caught before Jesus is fully revealed. In other words, this is our mission *before* every eye will see Him. A less-than-fully-revealed Christ directs the harvest of sheep nations, and that will be the last effort we will be involved with before we see Him as clearly as we are seen. Interestingly, not all disciples will have been involved in this great catch. In John 21, nearly half of them were home sleeping while these seven were interacting with the Lord in their catch. To apply this as a parable, this means that many will not be involved in the rescuing of nations. Some of Jesus' true disciples will be under the sleep of a wrong view of the End Times that caters to weak faith. In fact, it is probably the weak faith that engenders a wrong eschatology. Correct eschatology says, "Jesus is not going to fully reveal Himself until we have caught a large haul of *nations*—not individuals within nations—so that must be where we put our effort." We must believe that even while it is very dark and even though we haven't yet seen entire nations come into the kingdom net, this is our very real destiny. We must be preparing a kingdom-sized mesh with strong material that will hold "large fish" and not break.

If we aim discipleship efforts only at individuals, we will have a net designed only to catch small things and unable to sustain a catch of nations. We'd better be preparing for a harvest of entire nations, which means we need discipleship material that is applicable at a nation level. That's what the seven mountain template provides.

ANOTHER 153

Matthew 25 establishes that "sheep nations" will be on the right. John 21 suggests that there will be 153 of them—large fish that were caught on the right side of the boat. Why 153? Does that number carry special significance, or is that just the number of nations that will happen to respond? Will the political lines of nations so change that this number might one day represent *all* nations? I don't know. I preach and teach that we shouldn't give up on any nation. Psalm 2:8 doesn't say, "Ask of Me the nations for an inheritance—except for this one over here and that one over there." I don't believe it has been foreordained for any nation to be evil and therefore destroyed. Even the destruction of nations that come against Israel is not to be seen as an unavoidable script but a warning to nations not to go down that path. Scripture is clear that even if a sentence is determined against an individual or a nation, that judgment can be reversed through repentance. Therefore, any nation can become a "sheep nation." The invitation is to all. Though rebellion is more entrenched in some than in others, all can theoretically go in any direction. The key is whether Jesus' disciples are fishing for the nations while it's night.

I have found only one other Scripture passage that refers to the number 153. When 2 Kings 1 begins, Elijah has crushed Queen Jezebel and embarrassed her god, Baal, and even King Ahab has died. The king of Israel sends three different captains with 50 men each to command Elijah to come down from the top of the mountain. Elijah tells the first captain and his 50 men that if he is a man of God, fire will come down from heaven and consume the captain and his men. Because Elijah is a man of God, that's exactly what happened. This is repeated two more times, with the exception that the last captain and his men are spared because the captain pleads for mercy. Three captains with 50 men each makes a total of 153. I suggest that this can't be a coincidence as we connect it to the fishing for nations in John 21.

Furthermore, it isn't long before Elijah ascends into heaven, which takes place in the next chapter—perhaps an eschatological clue. The subtitle of my previous book, *The Seven Mountain Prophecy,* is "Unveiling the Coming Elijah Revolution." According to Malachi 4:5–6, Elijah must come before the day of the Lord and turn the hearts of fathers to their children and the hearts of the children to their fathers. This is the last word of the Old Testament. The day of the Lord will be "great" *and* "dreadful." It will be the best of times and the worst of times. You get to choose whether to be on the great or dreadful side of things by whom you show allegiance to.

> Now it shall come to pass in the latter days that the mountain of the LORD's house shall be established on the top of the mountains, and shall be exalted above the hills; and all nations shall flow to it.
>
> —ISAIAH 2:2

The eschatology we can extract from 2 Kings 1 speaks of this day when an Elijah revolution, characterized by a refusal to compromise with Jezebel and Baal, sweeps through the earth. The mountain of celebration, where Jezebel has operated, and the mountain of family, where Baal has operated, will now be under Elijah's influence. He will be the one sitting on the top of the mountain, but world governments are not yet ready to let him fully reign. The captain sent by the king instructed Elijah, "Man of God, come down! You have too much authority and influence, and you have to come down from your high place." This will be the last resistance nations will show to the establishment of the Lord's house on the tops of the mountains. I believe that 102 "sheep nations" (represented by the first two units of 50 men and their captains; see 2 Kings 1) will need some fire to convince them to become sheep, but that 51 will voluntarily recognize that the authority from God's house is higher than their own.

In 2 Kings 1, Elijah only comes down from the mountain to rebuke the king for inquiring of an idol.

> Then he said to him, "Thus says the LORD: 'Because you have sent messengers to inquire of Baal-Zebub, the god of Ekron, is it because there is no God in Israel to inquire of His word? Therefore you shall not come down from the bed to which you have gone up, but you shall surely die.'"
>
> —2 KINGS 1:16

After his warning to the king, Elijah is then done with his mission on earth, and is taken by whirlwind into heaven (2 Kings 2:1).

Baal-Zebub (Beelzebub) is the principality that releases humanism in all its various poses. The governments that insist in operating from this foundation will surely die.

As we noted, 150 soldiers followed the fate of their respective lead captains. I believe that the "three captains" could be speaking of the U.S., China, and India. These three nations represent nearly three billion people, and each one exercises great sway on other nations. They are superpowers, or "captains" of nations. Two captains will have to be humbled by fire before they will submit to Elijah, but one will learn righteousness by observing the experience of the other two.

> For when Your judgments are in the earth, the inhabitants of the world will learn righteousness.
>
> —ISAIAH 26:9

THE NEW 7M DISCIPLESHIP

The coming changes on the mountain of religion will revolutionize the church. Discipleship will be redefined. What we have considered discipleship is in fact very watered down from what true discipleship is. Becoming a true disciple will entail understanding God's ways in the seven primary sectors of society. We will learn and instruct in the sevenfold Spirit of God. Individual discipleship will be redefined by this, and then we will add to our mission the discipling of nations.

THE HOME CHURCH MOVEMENT

The exploding home church movement has positives and negatives to it. Much of it comes in response to the weak, ineffectual state of many traditional churches. The movement reflects the fact that many are done with "religion" and church as usual. It's a search for true, authentic Christianity. Ritualistic, passive, Sunday-morning church is just not cutting it anymore. Pastors and leaders who have to pressure people into attending and tithing are going to continue to lose their voice and their place.

Church membership is meant to be much more than just being strong-armed into attending, tithing, and volunteering to serve. Any church where there is no manifest presence of God is just a plantation. So is any church where you are not being trained, equipped, and released for ministry on the seven mountains. I don't believe that you have to pray about leaving plantations. You just do it unless specifically directed by God not to. But most churches don't equip people to recognize His voice, so getting that direction is difficult. Even so, many feel led by God to leave traditional churches for home churches.

One of the downsides of the home church movement is that some of it seems to be born from an orphan spirit. The orphan spirit says, "If no one is going to take care of me, I'm going to take care of myself." A certain aspect of that could be all right, but those operating from this spirit usually feel done with spiritual parents. Ironically, the lack of being under proper spiritual parenting leads people to choose even less parenting. This orphan spirit makes home churches seedbeds for a Lone Ranger mentality. It can easily turn into the spiritual equivalent of living together—no-commitment Christianity that carries the lawless spirit of this age.

The great need in this coming season will be true authority, not *no* authority. We will need more spiritual moms and pops, not less. True apostles and pastors are about to rise to meet the need of this generation and manifest the truth of Malachi 4:6. They will be fathers whose hearts are turned to their sons, true spiritual parents whose greatest joy will be to see their sons and daughters grow and take their places. These parents won't necessarily be called or even officially recognized as fathers and mothers, but they will function in that role. They will collectively provide an atmosphere of healthy family dynamics within the church.

The enemy would love to preempt the rising of spiritual fathers and mothers by closing down the hearts of "children" through past negative experiences and negative connotations. This would cause children to provide parenting for each other because their hearts are already closed to true parental instruction. But God's healing, restorative work in this day will also turn the hearts of children to their fathers and mothers. There will be multiple manifestations of this in other sectors of society, but it will certainly manifest in the house of the Lord. Coming healthy churches and movements will gather around true godly authority.

God is removing "tares"—pseudo-leaders who suck life out of members of the body—so that great spiritual parents can be showcased. The broken personal life of false leaders is eventually revealed because their spiritual authority isn't real. A tare is a plant that has the appearance of real fruit-bearing grain but really only feeds itself. It can even have pretend fruit, but it is not the kind of fruit that remains. Spiritual tares can fake fruitfulness too, but it's all appearance.

> Therefore as the tares are gathered and burned in the fire, so it will be at the end of this age. The Son of Man will send out His angels, and they will gather out of His kingdom all things that offend, and those who practice lawlessness, and will cast them into the furnace of fire. There will be wailing and gnashing of teeth. Then the righteous will shine forth as the sun in the kingdom of their Father. He who has ears to hear, let him hear!
> —Matthew 13:40–43, emphasis added

I want to take a fresh look at Jesus' parable of the wheat and tares and perhaps help you see it in a new way. The tares are gathered out of *His kingdom*. In Matthew 13:38, Jesus explains that "the field is the world" and that the kingdom is made up of "the sons of the kingdom." What could possibly be gathered from His kingdom that would then cause the righteous to shine like the sun? I believe this is speaking of false leaders who are sown by Satan in unique ways. They have said the sinner's prayer and may even make it into heaven. (I believe that the furnace of fire process is for believers who make it in "so as through fire," as 1 Corinthians 3:15 puts it.) They are sown by Satan in the sense that Satan recognizes people with great cracks in their foundation and knows how to sabotage them. These tares are practically guaranteed to be future scandal-makers. They are wounded, and their character is compromised; and Satan assists to artificially pump up something destined to blow up and disparage the kingdom of God. These leaders carry what seems like a true anointing but in fact is a Jezebel anointing. I've witnessed many such tares recently—those whom many considered to be highly anointed but later discovered that their "anointing" was a spiritual additive Satan mixed up for them.

We are in a season when God is releasing the angels who will gather the tares of false leadership out of His kingdom. This is a necessary work of the Lord among us so that the righteous, the coming Josephs, can "shine like the sun." A manifestation of God's children will be seen on earth, and we will be as dominant a feature as the sun is. This work of gathering angels won't always be made evident by scandals, as these angels will work to preempt the scandals that Satan has attempted through his tares. Many of these scandals will be observed within the Christian arena but will not extend into the world's news radar. Unusual deaths and resignations will be one manifestation of the work of these gathering angels. That doesn't mean that we should assume deaths and resignations to be the result of angels weeding out the kingdom, but this is one way God will make room for His true shepherds to properly oversee His flock. The intensity of the coming days makes it imperative to have spiritually mature and discerning leadership in its proper place.

Mountain-Specific Churches

The mountain of religion will begin to explode with new manifestations of out of the box churches. Many mountain-specific churches will begin to arise. There will be mountain of education churches that focus entirely on affecting that sector of society. There will be mountain of celebration churches whose entire focus will be invading the arts and entertainment sector of society and demonstrating the greater glory that God has available for those who will look to Him. There will be churches that adapt to each of the mountains and enable their members to emphasize that face of God.

This seven mountain orientation will greatly increase our effectiveness in displacing the darkness at the head of society. Similarly "mountained" churches will be able to cooperate in conferences and projects to bring great synergy and power to what is coming out of God's house.

The Coming Costliness of Idolatry

Idolatry is one of the primary issues for us to instruct people about in the future. God will increasingly release geography-specific judgments for idolatry, and we must partner with Him in helping people understand what's taking place. The Lord views idolatry as cheating on Him, and He is a jealous lover. All idolatry will ultimately be a target for His wrath—the wrath of a spurned lover who has given everything to redeem us but has been repeatedly rejected. Anyone hanging on to an idol will be in danger of receiving the judgment intended for the idol.

God speaks directly about idolatry after the promise in Isaiah 2:2 of His house being exalted as head:

> Their land is also full of idols; they worship the work of their own hands, that which their own fingers have made. People bow down, and each man humbles himself; therefore do not forgive them. Enter into the rock, and hide in the dust, from the terror of the LORD and the glory of His majesty. The lofty looks of man shall be humbled, the haughtiness of men shall be bowed down, and the LORD alone shall be exalted in that day....But the idols He shall utterly abolish....In that day a man will cast away his

idols of silver and his idols of gold, which they made, each for himself to worship, to the moles and bats, to go into the clefts of the rocks, and into the crags of the rugged rocks, from the *terror of the* LORD *and the glory of His majesty,* when He arises to shake the earth mightily.

—ISAIAH 2:8–11, 18, 20–21, EMPHASIS ADDED

"The glory of His majesty" and "the terror of the Lord" will operate simultaneously. If you turn to Him, you will be exposed to the glory of His majesty. If you stay in idolatry, you will reap the terror of the Lord.

The mountain of religion will receive an extreme makeover as the Lord's Josephs arise and step into their rightful place, carrying His mantle of favor. All other mountains will flow from this one as the house of the Lord is exalted and established in the last days. The nation of Israel and the city of Jerusalem will be an integral part of this great End Time work. Israel will be the Lord's anvil upon which the destiny of all other nations is being formed. It will be impossible to be a sheep nation and not understand Jerusalem's central role of restoration. The Lord will not rest until He has made Jerusalem a praise before all nations (Isa. 62:7). The process will be fiery, but it will also be glorious.

19

And All Nations Came to Joseph

As the Lord was fast-forwarding Joseph's rise to societal influence, He was also preparing the challenges that would force all nations to turn to the solutions that were in His favorite son.

Moreover He called for a famine in the land; He destroyed all the provision of bread. He sent a man before them—Joseph— who was sold as a slave.

—Psalm 105:16–17

It is imperative that we be like the sons of Issachar and understand the times. The Lord will be simultaneously doing two things. First he will raise up His Josephs to invade the seven mountains of society, and then He will intervene to cause current systems to begin failing. He will raise up the solution while bringing about the problems that cause society to be drawn to the anointing on the sons of light.

The famine was over all the face of the earth, and Joseph opened all the storehouses and sold to the Egyptians. And the famine became severe in the land of Egypt. So all countries came to Joseph in Egypt to buy grain, because the famine was severe in all lands.

—Genesis 41:56–57

God has not lost His sovereignty among the affairs of human beings. He can still call for a famine in the land. This famine may be literal, but it could be a symbolic famine on the systems of this world. The mountain of economy has been under a God-ordered famine designed to surface a Joseph solution. He has gutted the operating generator of the world's economy, and He essentially did it in one day. In one fell swoop, the world realized that we had been living in economic la-la land. In an instant, we realized that we had been driven by unimaginable greed, and the world's behavior toward money changed.

God will cause the nations to run to the glory that shines through His children. His glory will be seen on us. Entire nations will be able to be rescued, but they will have to yield to the light that is on the sons and daughters of God (Isa. 60:1–3). The nations that will not recognize and turn to their Josephs will suffer catastrophic losses and tragedies.

To complicate matters and cause us to misread the times, Satan has attempted to undermine the world economy, too. His motivation, of course, is entirely different than that of God, who desires the nations as His inheritance. Satan's purpose is death, destruction, mayhem, starvation, violence, war, etc. It's what he does and looks for opportunities to do. He's a weakener and destroyer of nations. Before September 2008, his plan was in full operation. He was strengthening the economies of Antichrist-hosting nations (through oil prices), and he had so sped up the world economy through Mammon (greed) that a devastating, catastrophic crash would have been inevitable. The Lord intervened, slowing down the economy with a thud and changing the nature of the crisis.

It can be confusing to decipher this matter by natural observation because the most powerful forces on earth are targeting the same mountain. One seeks destruction, and one wants to provide a rescue through a Joseph. One wants the earth to be filled with his vile hatred, and one wants the earth filled with His glory. Both want to kill anything in us that tries to make it apart from their resources.

Let me offer a helpful hint for those of you feeling the crunch of this predicament of superpowers wanting to "kill" you: yield to the one who has already secured a full, glorious victory. His name is Alpha and Omega. He is the beginning and the end. Whatever judgment He sends your way is to separate you from the inferior solutions that the deceiver is offering. It is our God's great pleasure to shower us with extravagant provision. He just insists that we go to His bank—which is Himself—and not to Satan's greed-driven bank. Satan's bank carries profound interest penalties that, when you've read all the fine print, leave you in worse shape than when you first went to him. God's provision has no sorrow added to it. Many Christians are struggling because we have given lip service to God and His bank, all the while doing business with Satan's bank. God's judgment on Satan's bank is not designed to harm His children, but you will experience the consequences if that's where you have been banking.

This principle is true for all seven mountains. God loves manifesting true government. He loves exalting good news. He loves to showcase the glory of His creativity, to reveal His wisdom and understanding, to establish the proper relational interplay of families, to provide for His children, and to create a culture of honor. All these represent manifestations of God on the seven mountains of society. He wants you to see all aspects of His face.

As God's child, you will only feel His coming judgment to the degree you are "in bed" with the seven distortions of Satan. He models government through pride and corruption. He mixes news with gossip, slander, and fear. He twists creativity to showcase distorted sensuality and death. He perverts family through unnatural and forced unions. He counterfeits provision through fear-based avarice. He attempts to steal worship through artificial constructs of religiosity. Any shaking God brings to your life is to separate you from Satan's counterfeit web of deceit, and any shaking He brings to nations is for the same purpose. He knows that He Himself is the desire of the nations if they are not under this web of deception. Therefore, He must deal ruthlessly with the deception.

Ultimately, the goodness of God will be vindicated. He is so intensely devoted to you and me that He will stop at nothing to win us to Himself. He will let His own present-day reputation suffer for us to have a chance later to see what He was doing all along. This principle is also true at a national level. He is so intensely in love with and devoted to all nations that He will risk His present reputation in an attempt to rescue them from long-term harm. By that I mean He will allow disciplines and judgments so that a long-term good may be secured for a nation. Some will temporarily perceive Him to be a stern, judging God, but His mercy exceeds even His need for an immediate good reputation.

In His amazing End Times plan, God will raise up His seeing sons and daughters and allow them to shine brighter than the sun with answers and solutions for the world to see how heaven can function on earth. Heaven has all seven mountain realities. The Spirit of God is running through the earth looking for the Josephs who will let Him reveal His glorious solutions for mankind through them. More than anyone, He wants world peace. But He also knows we are not going to get it doing business with Satan's institutions. The End Times will be known by the open bankruptcy of Satan's counterfeit kingdoms and the establishment of the legitimate kingdoms of our God. The rule and reign of God will descend to earth, and that is the big deal of the Last Days. The Antichrist will not be the big deal. The beast will not be the big deal. The false prophet will not be the big deal. They will all be microscopic compared to Him who sits on the throne of glory and compared to His plan scripted for these amazing Last Days.

> Look among the nations and watch—be utterly astounded! For
> I will work a work in your days which you would not believe,
> though it were told you.
>
> —HABAKKUK 1:5

Get ready to have your mind blown. Not one of us has even dreamed of the wondrous things God is going to pull off. We are all going to be "utterly astounded." The things I've been telling you in this book, even if you're struggling to believe them, are the bare minimum. The grandeur of what is actually coming will far surpass anything I'm saying. I don't yet have sufficient faith to stretch into seeing what He's going to do. It will outdo anything Hollywood could ever think of. If He were to tell us, we wouldn't believe it, so He's just going to surprise us. He's going to blow our minds *before* He takes us somewhere. He doesn't need to change the entire rules of operation to get this done. He doesn't need to cheat to pull this off. He is going to use little old you and little old me. Even the twenty-four elders are going to fall off their chairs from what they see (Rev. 4:10; 5:8). God is going to cause all creation to be wonderstruck with what He has done.

20

2015 and Beyond

THIS BOOK HAS focused mainly on the seven-year period from Rosh Hashanah 2008 to Rosh Hashanah 2015. This is a specific season in which the Lord is raising up His Josephs and placing on them a mantle of His favor to bring solutions to entire nations. But this is just the beginning. God will continue working well beyond 2015.

THE SUDDEN UNPLUGGING OF THE WORLD'S SYSTEMS

Starting with Rosh Hashanah of 2015, a seismic shift will take place in the same way that the seven years of plenty ended in Egypt. If a great earthquake happens that day, consider it the Lord's grace clearly signaling that earth-rattling changes are upon us. On this day, there will be a great unplugging of the systems of this world. The Lord will call for a famine on the foundations that are not sourced from His kingdom. It will be a significant manifestation—if not *the* definitive manifestation—of a well-known passage in Hebrews:

> See that you do not refuse Him who speaks. For if they did not escape who refused Him who spoke on earth, much more shall we not escape if we turn away from Him who speaks from heaven, whose voice then shook the earth; but now He has promised, saying, "Yet once more I shake not only the earth, but also heaven." Now this, "Yet once more," indicates the removal of those things that are being shaken, as of things that are made, that the things which cannot be shaken may remain. Therefore,

since we are receiving a kingdom which cannot be shaken, let us have grace, by which we may serve God acceptably with reverence and godly fear. For our God is a consuming fire.

—HEBREWS 12:25–29

God will speak from heaven, and His voice will make a quantum penetration into the subatomic structures of the planet to shake everything that can be shaken. He will initiate the next level of shaking of world systems in order to ultimately establish His kingdom as the unshakeable asset of the last days. Nations will have garnered earthquake insurance to the degree that Joseph strategies have been implemented at nationwide levels. His kingdom is an unshakeable system, and anything that is constructed with kingdom solutions will be unshakeable.

Just as Egypt hardly felt the shift into famine, it will be possible for us to hardly feel the coming earthquake. The key was and still is whether Josephs are in place. If Joseph had not prepared Egypt during seven years of plenty, the country and those around it would have been devastated. All nations had to respond to the new realities, but some were in better shape than others. It is safe to say that all existing society in that part of the world could have faced extinction without Joseph in place. The famine was so severe that it made everyone forget the previous abundance. The nations were under gross darkness, but heaven's intentions were that His glory could be seen on His Joseph (Isa. 60:1–3).

The future famine may not compare identically with the famine of Joseph's day. There may or may not be physical drought and famine. The primary famine will be that societal generators will be unplugged and former systems will cease to function properly. There will be a seven mountain collapse of all that does not proceed from the house of God. Humanistic educational systems will be proven totally bankrupt. Mammon-based economic structures will catastrophically fail. Artistic manifestations from the spirit of Jezebel will experience a widespread collapse in appeal and a total collapse in funding. People will turn on their idols with a vengeance as eyes begin to be opened to the web of lies undergirding false religions. Unprecedented family violence and disintegration will show up in cultures that have venerated false gods. The gods will turn on them because their gods are demons. News viewership will take an amazing turn as people shift en masse to credible news reporting. Though there has already been a trend in this direction, the sudden turn in world events will convince people of whose reporting can be trusted and whose can't. Governments that have not previously been fortified with preemptive Joseph people and plans will collapse almost overnight. Nations without the sons and daughters of God in positions of light will become ungovernable as never before.

The seven-year period leading up to Rosh Hashanah 2015 will have revealed splashes of the kingdom, but splashes will turn to full-fledged movements after that. People, get ready—God's kingdom really is coming, and it will incrementally shake existing structures as it nears full implementation. We who are His children are the receivers of His kingdom. We are to be the unshakeable element of future days. We are currently going through mini test runs of what will be our new reality. Those without Christ will run to those anchored in Christ, because we will be on the only unshakeable ground.

This will not be a time to fear if you are a child and servant of God. This shaking will lead us into our greatest hour. Nations will walk to the light of the children of the one true, living God. According to prophecy, nations will stream to the mountain of the house of God: "'I will shake all nations, and they shall come to the Desire of All Nations, and I will fill this temple with glory,' says the LORD of hosts" (Hag. 2:7). This is the original Old Testament word that is echoed in Hebrews 12. God is going to shake all nations, and this shaking is not to destroy them but to cause them to properly recognize He who is: the Desire of all nations. He gives Himself that name. He loves nations and knows that nations were created to love Him. Sheep nations will love Him at a nationwide level. This goes well beyond just ethnic groups within nations loving Him well.

MIGHT ALL NATIONS BECOME "SHEEP"?

Earlier I laid out a case for 153 countries becoming sheep nations. This in itself takes great faith and can stretch our ability to hope. I want to now make a case for *all* countries becoming sheep nations by putting together two passages of Scripture: Exodus 4:22–23 and Romans 11:16.

Then you shall say to Pharaoh, "Thus says the LORD: 'Israel is My son, My firstborn. So I say to you, let My son go that he may serve Me. But if you refuse to let him go, indeed I will kill your son, your firstborn.'"

—EXODUS 4:22–23

In this first passage, Moses receives his original instruction to command Pharaoh to let God's people go. The wording then is very interesting. Moses was to tell Pharaoh that Israel was His firstborn. This has tremendous implications that still reverberate today. First, it establishes that God looks at nations as His children. We have to get this, even if it requires us to develop a new grid of understanding. "Israel is My son, My firstborn." Can you imagine looking at an entire nation as your child? Can you imagine having hopes and dreams for a nation like we have for our own children? God wanted Pharaoh to be aware that this is how He thought. "Israel is My firstborn, and if you don't let Israel go, I'm going to kill your firstborn son." The final plague against the Egyptians was for them to feel God's pain for His firstborn. God kept upping the ante on His judgments until Pharaoh finally got it. He was no more likely to give up on Israel—a stiff-necked, rebellious Israel, mind you—than Pharaoh would ever consider giving up on his firstborn. This is why God will *never* give up on the nation of Israel. They are His firstborn nation, and He just can't do that. He'll allow all kinds of refining trials and fires to come so that they come to a proper relationship with Him, but He will not rest until He has made Jerusalem a praise in all the earth.

Israel My *First*born

Not only does God look at the nation of Israel as a son, He also sees Israel as His *first* son. All the way back in Exodus, this nation was just the first, not the only. God clearly intended to have more "children"—nations that He viewed as sons—that He would go to the ends of the world to redeem, that He would personally war against principalities over. He will not be happy only to rescue His firstborn. Many are teaching that limited view—that Israel will be saved and all other nations will be destroyed—as a foundational part of their eschatological understanding. But God never calls Israel His only child. It's his first among others.

If Israel is God's firstborn, how many other children is He going to have? How many of the nations will He fight for? Could He possibly go after *all* nations? Let's look at the second passage, from Romans 11.

For if their being cast away is the reconciling of the world, what will their acceptance be but life from the dead? For if the first-fruit is holy, the lump is also holy; and if the root is holy, so are the branches.

—ROMANS 11:15–16

The Principle of the Firstfruit

The above verse is based on the scriptural principle of firstfruits. If the firstfruit/firstborn is holy, then the whole lump is also holy. Here in Romans, Paul is specifically speaking of Israel as the firstfruit nation through whom all nations are granted potential sonship. Reconciliation was made available for the world.

I know we are used to applying this at a personal level, but God is clearly not talking at that level. He is not speaking of Abraham and only matters of personal salvation but of Israel and of salvation being made available to Gentile nations—not just the individuals of the nations but the nations themselves. I realize that this stretches the beliefs of a lot of people, but we need to get stretched to fit biblical foundations, even if it seems impossible. We are not given the prerogative to choose only believable possibilities of Scripture. Don't let your unbelief negate the possibility that all nations will voluntarily come as sons and enter into a loving relationship with the Father. If the firstfruit is holy, then the whole lump is holy. God is going after the whole lump.

What else could David have been seeing in Psalm 22?

All the ends of the world shall remember and turn to the LORD, and all the families of the nations shall worship before You. For the kingdom *is* the LORD's, and He rules over the nations.

—PSALM 22:27–28

And then again in Psalm 72?

Yes, all kings shall fall down before Him; all nations shall serve Him.

—PSALM 72:11

"Ah," you say, "that is during the Millennium, the time period we assign for all 'unbelievable' things of Scripture to take place." Whatever we have no faith for is almost automatically thrown into the Millennium in our minds—as if there will be a new set of rules in operation under which people will no longer have free choice, and, therefore, good things are possible. But the context of Psalm 72 shows us differently. After it says that "all nations will serve Him," it describes conditions of this age:

> For he will deliver the needy when he cries, the poor also, and him who has no helper. He will spare the poor and needy. He will redeem their life from oppression and violence; And precious shall be their blood in His sight.
>
> —PSALM 72:12–14

This hardly seems like a millennial setting. Needy people are crying, there are poor and helpless people, there is violence and oppression, and blood is being shed. Yet in this same age, government leaders will fall down before Him—*all* kings, to be specific. Before rules of the Millennium get implemented, God is going to do an amazing thing through His sons and daughters.

It's clear that He will not do this work unilaterally. Two verses later, the psalm says, "There will be an abundance of grain in the earth, on the top of the mountains" (Ps. 72:16). This speaks of Josephs being in their places! There will be famine, violence, and difficulty elsewhere, but at the tops of the mountains there will be abundance of provision. From that which flows from the tops of the mountains, God will take care of the poor and needy who cry out to Him. He is doing this grand finale with His collaborating Josephs. He will subdue the nations under *our* feet (Ps. 47:3). He will be exalted among the nations (Ps. 46:10).

> Oh, let the nations be glad and sing for joy! For You shall judge the people righteously, and govern the nations on earth.
>
> —PSALM 67:4

God isn't just going to strong-arm nations into subjection. He is going to govern them. He will manifest His way of governing nations here on earth through His Josephs at the tops of the mountains. I must continuously emphasize that these will be Josephs as opposed to just Christians in general. The "sons of Leah" will never be a part of this great work. They will be joyous recipients of the blessings that come from the Josephs, but they themselves will not be the instruments of government here on earth. Their eschatological presuppositions never allowed them to dream Father's dreams, so they therefore never received the mantle of favor to displace the darkness on the tops of the mountains.

I believe at least 153 nations will respond to God, but He has designs for all nations: "Arise, O God, judge the earth; For you shall inherit all nations" (Ps. 82:8). Israel was His firstborn, and He wants *all* of His children. Perhaps as things progress and borders and nations are absorbed, there may only be 153 nations. However it actually works out, we must know that God is going to go after every single nation as if it were one of His children. He will plead with them to abandon allegiance to Lucifer. God will prove to them that Lucifer is an illegitimate parent and only interested in their destruction. It may be a shocking paradigm for some to embrace, but God will allow many people to die in judgment if it will turn a nation to Him. It is clearly not His preference for it to have to happen this way, but it is a way He will go. His ways are not our ways, and neither are His thoughts like our thoughts— until we come in line with His dreams. Of course we must realize that His love for nations is also definitely associated with the fact that nations are made up of people. God will save individuals on the basis of their faith in Jesus Christ, regardless of the nation they come from.

There is glory on a nation that properly functions on earth. This glory reveals the characteristics of God like nothing else can. His glory will only fill the earth when it is refracted through the lenses of nations under His governance. God is too great and marvelous to be painted only on the canvas of individuals. If He is not revealed through nations, He is not really understood and therefore not truly worshiped.

If you can't see God at work through nations, you are only interacting with your perception of who God is and not with who He really is. That may get you into heaven, but you will be at least figuratively weeping and gnashing teeth when you become fully aware of what the picture was and what your role was supposed to be. You will, of course, be thankful and joyful that you are permitted to live in heaven. He will let you in even if you buried the treasure of your destiny. But your joy will be tinged, as it were, with weeping and gnashing of teeth when you realize you didn't see what He was doing and therefore had no faith to be a part of His magnificent work among the nations. You will realize that you embraced sophisticated doctrines of doubt that permitted you to stay relatively asleep.

The rapture doctrine, as it is commonly expressed, is one of those sophisticated doctrines of doubt. When we have little faith that God could reform and transform society using us, we embrace a theology of escapism. This theology somehow trumps scores of scriptures that say the opposite. It sells books and movies by the millions, probably because it's more comfortable for most of us to validate our doubt and unbelief than repent of it. Distinguished theologians then reinforce escape theology so they themselves are not faced with their faithlessness. I'm being strong here because I'm stirred against the deception itself. I am not mentioning any specific theologian—I don't want to demean or judge any specific person. I'm sure many proponents of escapist theology have had demonstrated strong faith and character in certain areas and did well for the light they had received. Yet I am strongly opposed to the deception that causes them to despise Josephs and elaborately "conspire to kill" those who dream Papa's dreams. Meanwhile, creation itself groans and labors with birth pangs, eagerly waiting for the promised glory that reveals the mantled sons of God (Rom. 8:18–22). Nations and everything God has created know that when we get free, they will get free (Rom. 8:21). There is a glorious liberty to be attained when the kingdom comes on earth as it is in heaven.

How and When Does It All End?

I don't pretend to have all the prophetic answers about how and when End Time events happen. I'm sure I will be surprised with many of the twists and turns I haven't foreseen. I don't know if the seven-year period up to 2015 is the ultimate defining period for the manifestation of God's revealed sons, the Josephs. We are clearly in some final stage of birth pangs, but there still could be more. I believe we are at least in the crowning stage of the next kingdom age. We are in a seven-year period when what is coming will be upon us. By the time the year 2015 is over, I believe we will have that new kingdom baby among us.

Having said that, I think it's important to make this disclaimer: the purpose of this book is not so much to give an accurate timetable of coming events, but to be accurate in the scope of coming events. Prophesying precise timing is always difficult because eternity happens outside of the framework of human time and within the framework of heaven's time. Prophetic delays and acceleration are always possibilities. That isn't an excuse, just a reality. God, the ultimate prophet who cannot lie, prophesied over Moses that he and all Israel would be taken by Him to the Promised Land. No one but Joshua and Caleb made it, and it was forty years late. Joshuas and Calebs are always around to accelerate destiny, and "ten spies" are always around to delay it.

When God prophesies destiny, it is always going to happen. The negotiable parts are always going to be "when" and "by whom." All the matters of victorious destiny that I have elaborated on in this book will in fact come about. I even believe that the timing will bear out to be true. But if you happen to be reading this book in 2030 and it just now seems like these Joseph possibilities are manifesting, then still believe it all and move in confidence. Sometimes seven years takes twenty years. For Israel, a ten-day trip took forty years. I don't for a moment believe that this kind of delay is likely, but my awareness of my humanity compels me to add this disclaimer in order not to lose the greater purpose of the book. Regardless of however long it takes and whomever God ultimately uses, this move of God is going to be utterly astounding. I think those days are on us now.

WE WILL SHINE LIKE THE SUN

The path of the just is like the shining sun, that shines ever brighter unto the perfect day.

—PROVERBS 4:18

Then the righteous will shine forth as the sun in the kingdom of their Father. He who has an ear to hear, let him hear!

—MATTHEW 13:43

Nations will come to your light, and kings to the brightness of your rising.

—ISAIAH 60:3, NAS

The righteous will shine "ever brighter," and the end of things is not doom and gloom but a new "perfect day." That's the future that awaits all who will be Josephs from the house of Rachel. We will burn with the coals of His very heart, and the shine will displace every level of darkness. The sun shines not in a closet, not in a church, and not in some enclosed confine, but over the nations. Nations and kings won't come to "this little light of mine;" they will come to shining suns/sons.

The Father wants His children to shine as the sun in His kingdom, which we know is coming to earth. It is not humility to say, "No, Lord, *You* do all the shining." It is disobedience. I have four daughters, and it would give me no joy for them to let me shine but not shine themselves. I want them to shine with the DNA that God put in them. Your Father wants you to shine with His DNA, which He placed in you. If you want to give glory to God, you actually have to have some to give. By and large, we have people with only fame who give glory to God. But fame doesn't displace darkness; glory does. When you have enough of this glory to measure, then yes, make sure to steer it back to Papa. But don't be so "humble" that you refuse to carry His glory. Don't refuse to shine. He's looking for suns and for sons. And if you'll let Him, He'll put a mantle of many colors on you.

God is offering a displacing favor and anointing to all of His sons and daughters. He wants to do this *together*. This is the great *co*-mission. It is under His leadership and sovereignty, but He wants us to "go therefore and make disciples of nations" with the very authority that He regained on the cross. He's looking for *co*-laborers, for those who are willing to find out what Jesus looks like coming out of them. This is a place of relational privilege for those who wish to see our God made famous in all the earth. He will ultimately be vindicated as an exceedingly good and exceedingly great God. These last days will conclusively verify how good and great He has always been. He will ultimately win through the relentlessness of His love. His love ultimately cannot fail, and He is looking for friends who will partner with Him in the ultimate vindication of His goodness and greatness.

Position yourself from this time forward to be one of His favorites. He's got a beautiful coat of many colors and the dreams that come with it. Rise up, Josephs—you have been called to save the age!

APPENDIX

The Seven Mountain Prophecy

B ECAUSE SO MUCH of the material in this book on the Joseph anointing expands on my previous book, *The Seven Mountain Prophecy: Unveiling the Coming Elijah Revolution*, I would highly recommend reading that volume. But for a basic understanding of the seven mountain approach, the following is a brief summary of that book.

The world and the church are in need of an extreme makeover. The coming Elijah Revolution—a move of God that will have all the characteristics of the ministry of Elijah—will have a powerful transforming effect on both the world and the church. It will prepare the way of the Lord before His return. According to Scripture, Jesus will sit at God's right hand until all of His enemies are put under His feet. The Elijah Revolution will accomplish this.

Just as God's people followed the ark of His presence into the Promised Land, so will our generation follow Jesus' ministry on earth in unfamiliar ways. Our promised land is the nations of the world, all of which rightfully belong to God. As the Lord brings us into this land, we will encounter seven nations "greater and mightier" than us (as in Deuteronomy 7:1). Joshua's enemies were the Hittites, the Girgashites, the Amorites, the Canaanites, the Perizzites, the Hivites, and the Jebusites. For us, those nations correspond to the seven "mountains" that shape society: media, government, education, economy, religion, celebration and arts, and family. With God-given strategies and power, Elijah revolutionaries will have unprecedented favor to displace the evil principalities on these mountains and occupy them with kingdom citizens.

THE MOUNTAIN OF MEDIA

The word *Hittite* comes from a word meaning "terror" and "fear"—exactly the characteristics of modern news media, which focuses overwhelmingly on negative news and even decides which negative stories get the most airtime and headlines. The principality Apollyon (meaning "destroyer"), who sits atop the mountain of media, twists news and enslaves people by magnifying their fears. Elijah revolutionaries, who will function essentially as true evangelists, will report news accurately, even when it's bad news, but will be able to find the redemptive angle in every story. Their words will powerfully prophesy the blessings of God to the world.

THE MOUNTAIN OF GOVERNMENT

Many Christians believe politics to be "of the devil." That's because Christians have abandoned this sector of society to the devil. The Girgashites, whose name means "dwelling in clay soil," represent the earthly desires and corrupt ambitions common to this mountain. Lucifer, the prince of this mountain, will be displaced by those who ascend it in a spirit opposite to his pride, a spirit of humility and service. True apostles—not those who have a business card that carries the title "apostle," but those who function in that role as Scripture defines it—will be instrumental in taking the mountain of government. They will understand that "of the increase of [Jesus'] government there will be no end" (Isa. 9:7).

THE MOUNTAIN OF EDUCATION

Highly influential educational institutions that began centuries ago as Christian colleges and universities are now saturated in liberal, humanistic philosophies. The mountain of education is dominated by schools like Harvard, Yale, and Princeton, each of which has educated numerous world leaders. The Amorites on this mountain, who represent pride, boasting, and haughtiness, characterize the man-exalting ideals of humanism, liberalism, rationalism, and atheism. God's judgments will soon be clear enough that people will stop wondering if there is a God and ask instead what they should do about His existence.

A prevailing flaw in all educational systems is the emphasis on left-brain understanding of truth. Extreme prejudice against right-brain ways of thinking transform the vast majority of children from those who are able to receive creative, imaginative, intuitive revelation from God to those who are rationalistic, critical, and so limited to the five senses that they can't receive God's revelation. The Elijah Revolution will dethrone Beelzebub from this mountain, turn education back to a right brain-dominant enterprise, and open the way for children to discern the presence of God and prophesy His mysteries.

THE MOUNTAIN OF ECONOMY

The twin lies of greed and poverty both grow out of the influence of the principalities of Mammon, or Babylon. This lying spirit convinces people everywhere that money is their true source of provision. It prefers to enslave people in poverty, but where God blesses with abundance, it twists abundance into greed for more. But the economic systems of this world will one day collapse, and all who have operated under this spirit of poverty and greed will be left with nothing to depend on except God.

God calls His people to come out of this system. Those who depend exclusively on Him will "eat the wealth of nations." Abundance will come as a result of faith in the prophetic words God gives through His servants—a dynamic demonstrated often in Scripture (through men like Joseph, Elijah, and Elisha) and in my own experiences in Honduras, Costa Rica, Peru, and elsewhere.

Babylon will be shaken until it collapses, but those who trust in the Lord will suffer no lack.

The Mountain of Religion

Idolatry strips people of their provision and protection—words that reflect the meaning of the Perizzites' name—by placing them in submission to gods that can't and won't deliver on their empty promises. The spirit of religion atop the mountain of religion does everything it can to steal worship that rightfully belongs to God, whether through blatant worship of Satan, subtle religiosity within the church, or anything in between. This spirit distorts our worship with lying doctrines that seem true but are mixed with poison. Even mature Christians can stall out in their worship by focusing on a mountaintop experience or exalting a doctrine over a real relationship with God.

This mountain can only be taken through the dynamic leading and power of the Holy Spirit. Elijah revolutionaries will expect the Spirit to work in unexpected ways and be sensitive to His voice. Wildly, passionately in love with the Lord, they will refuse to practice a religion based on platitudes and principles, well-scheduled worship services, and neat and tidy theology. They will instead have supernatural experiences with God that defy the expectations and traditions of status quo Christianity.

The Mountain of Celebration

The mountain of celebration includes the arts, music, sports, fashion, entertainment, and every other way we celebrate and enjoy life. This mountain has so thoroughly been captured by Satan's hordes that most believers aren't sure it can even be possessed. But God's Spirit wants to move freely through the creativity and passion of His people. This mountain must be taken from the Hivites, who counterfeit true celebration with corrupt substitutes, and from the spirit of Jezebel, which seduces many away from the true pleasure and joy offered by God. The spirit of Jezebel prostitutes the good gifts of God, and the role of prophets will be to see through the deceptions of pop culture and offer the real and lasting alternative to our society, especially its youth, who live and breathe on this mountain during their teen years. Elijah revolutionaries will produce music, art, literature, and every other form of celebration the Lord's way—by being in His presence and letting His creativity flow through them. The world will begin to value and pursue the gift that Christian artists have because the quality of their work will point to a supernatural source.

THE MOUNTAIN OF FAMILY

Malachi promises that Elijah will come and "turn the hearts of the fathers to the children, and the hearts of the children to their fathers" (Mal. 4:6). It's the last promise—even the last verse—of the Old Testament. Elijah will come and save families. It's clear that families are under assault; we live in an era of unprecedented family breakdown. At the center of this problem is lack of fathers who are fully engaged in the life of their family. The results are numerous social and physical ills that spring out of rejection, including depression, fear, sexual deviance, addictions, anger, and violence.

The principality on this mountain is Baal, the worship of whom often involved sexual rituals and child sacrifice. The true role of pastors—in the marketplace, government (especially the judicial branch), as well as in churches—will be instrumental in removing Baal from the mountain of family and replacing him with functioning families who reflect the relationships within the Trinity and the family of God. We will receive and carry the restorative work of the spirit of Elijah to the nations.

THE HEAD AND NOT THE TAIL

It is important that we, God's blood-bought people, realize that it has always been His will for us to be at the top of the mountains in a place of preeminence and blessing. He is not a sadistic God who loves seeing His people struggle and barely survive. Nothing

141

could be further from the truth. He has always sought to motivate us with a promised land of unlimited abundance—body, soul, and spirit. He promised in Deuteronomy 28:13 to make His people "the head and not the tail."

For much of Christian history, the world has been the pacesetter, and the church has followed its forms by Christianizing secular music, art, government, business, and so on. The Elijah Revolution will change that. From the presence of God will flow superior ways of creating arts, conducting business, governing nations, and practicing faith and worship. The world will see the blessing of God on His people, and many will come to Christ from the scent of heaven that the church bears. Like Joshua and Caleb, Elijah revolutionaries will have a different spirit than the Christians who surrender the mountains of culture to the giants who live there. They will not be content to live in a Christian subculture that has little influence on society. They will zealously endeavor to bring entire nations into the kingdom of God.

For more information about Johnny Enlow, Daystar Church, and other Seven Mountain resources, go to:

www.DaystarAtlanta.org
www.SevenMountainProphecy.com

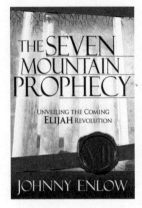

The coming Elijah Revolution will affect the entire world and will prepare the way of the Lord before His return. According to Scripture, Jesus will sit at God's right hand until all of His enemies are put under His feet. The Elijah Revolution will accomplish this as God's End-Time emissaries confront seven nations "greater and mightier than we"—the Hittites, Girgashites, Amorites, Canaanites, Perizzites, Hivites, and Jebusites. These nations correspond to seven "mountains" of global society—Media, Government, Education, Economy, Religion, Celebration/Arts, and Family.

With divine power and favor, revolutionaries will take these mountains for Christ! If you want to do your part, come now and be trained and equipped.

ISBN: 978-1-59979-287-3